BREAK
of
TIME

by *Hertha Pauli*

A Martin Dale Book

HAWTHORN BOOKS, INC.
Publishers
New York

BREAK OF TIME

English version copyright © 1972 by Hertha Pauli. German version, *Der Riss der Zeit geht durch mein Herz*, copyright © 1970 by Paul Zsolnay Verlag Gesellschaft m. b. H., Wien/Hamburg. Copyright under International and Pan-American Copyright Conventions. All rights reserved, including the right to reproduce this book, or portions thereof, in any form, except for the inclusion of brief quotations in a review. All inquiries should be addressed to Hawthorn Books, Inc., 70 Fifth Avenue, New York, New York 10011. This book was manufactured in the United States of America and published simultaneously in Canada by Prentice-Hall of Canada, Limited, 1870 Birchmount Road, Scarborough, Ontario. Library of Congress Catalog Card Number: 70-179113.

Type Design by Martin J. Baumann

1 2 3 4 5 6 7 8 9 10

The poems of Walter Mehring are from *Neues Ketzerbrevier*. All rights belong to Verlag Kiepenheuer & Witsch, Cologne, Germany. Quoted by permission. Translations by E. B. Ashton.

Author's Note

"The break of time cuts right through my heart," wrote the romantic poet Heinrich Heine about a century before we left Europe. The line came with us on the flight through France; my friend Walter Mehring, the modern poet, quoted it over and over.

"Did he know," he kept asking, "that this uncommon experience would become a common fate of our writers?"

I want this story of my own experiences to build a bridge, to link today with our yesterdays, my friends' and mine—a bridge of thoughts, memories, pictures, over the break of time.

H. P.

Contents

BREAK OF TIME

CHAPTER 1

Berlin Calling

In the days when Vienna was a metropolis, the capital of Hapsburg emperors and of Johann Strauss the Waltz King, its coffeehouses were the crossroads of a great society. There ideas were born, decisions reached, and hopes buried. The habitués, politicians, poets, or chess champions made their exits and their entrances on a miniature stage, mirroring the change in times.

The two most famous cafés of the good old days, the Herrenhof and the Central, faced each other near the former Imperial Palace. It was at the Herrenhof that Crown Prince Rudolf used to chat incognito with liberal journalists, and the goateed "Herr Bronstein" who played his daily chess games at the Central before World War I entered history afterward via America as Leon Trotsky.

I did not know that I would witness a historical moment when I went for a date with two friends at the Herrenhof

1

on Friday, March 11, 1938. I had been delayed at the Hotel Bristol by an American publisher's exciting interest in a new book of mine. Blanche Knopf was in town to meet Austrian authors, and my biography of the Austrian peace crusader Bertha von Suttner had already caused a minor storm: When I read a chapter from it on the Vienna radio (headed then by the brother of Chancellor Kurt von Schuschnigg), members of the outlawed Nazi party threw stink bombs at the broadcasting studio, and in Germany the book had been banned as fast as had my heroine's own half-century-old novel *Lay Down Arms*. Now Mrs. Knopf wished to take my controversial volume to New York with her, although the times seemed not propitious for pacifism.

From the Hotel Bristol on the Ring, Vienna's grand boulevard, you normally get to the Herrenhof in ten minutes. Not on that eleventh of March, though. "When the Ring is blocked, there's revolution," the Viennese have been saying since 1918. This time the police barricade had gone up because young Nazi hordes were demonstrating round the State Opera, bellowing, "Heil Hitler."

I turned back, looking indignantly for police protection. The first officer shrugged, but his partner—police like to go in pairs—suddenly turned on me. I ran, bewildered, and they followed, chasing me right into the mob, but the demonstrators let me pass because the police were after me. I managed to duck into a house, found another exit, and emerged across the street from the Herrenhof.

At the café the "Heil Hitler" chorus could be heard loud and clear. My friends looked relieved to see me. "The police have gone Nazi," I muttered to them, out of breath, and broke off when the waiter came to take my order as if nothing unusual were going on.

I had lost my appetite; all I wanted was "a cup of gold"—Viennese for coffee with cream—to steady my nerves while I talked with two kindred spirits. One, known as Carli, was a student and my partner in a literary agency we had named

2

Austrian Correspondence to identify it as the place for writers with an Austrian point of view. Today Dr. Carl Frucht is information officer for the United Nations World Health Organization in New Delhi.

Our third man was the exiled German poet Walter Mehring. He wrote lyrics and poetry in a new and special way and used to say that Bert Brecht had taken the format from him, not the other way round. In fact, Mehring had come to fame in Berlin before Bert Brecht had.

By 1934 Walter Mehring had come to Vienna from Paris to stay "for a few days," which had turned into a few years. Carli had called him right away to get him as a client for our agency, but Mehring had not returned the call. When we finally met at a party, he looked at me, wide-eyed, and started laughing. "*You* are Mrs. Austrian Correspondence?" He had been trying to dodge an official personage, not a palpably unofficial redhead wearing a hat with ribbons. Today —in print, on television, and in literary cafés from Berlin to Paris—Walter Mehring is still Walter Mehring.

"You'd better leave at once," I advised him at the Herrenhof. He had been a Nazi target for a decade, and Joseph Goebbels honored him with his personal wrath. Though never a party member of any sort, of all German refugees then in Vienna, Walter could least afford to be caught.

What was still called Austria, the German-speaking part remaining as an independent republic after the breakdown of the old Danube monarchy in 1918, was turning into very hot ground. Ever since 1918 there had been a movement postulating our "Anschluss"—our merging—with the German Reich. After Hitler became its Führer in 1933, only the Austrian Nazi party pursued that idea. Though officially pronounced "illegal," it was steadily growing, fed by German propaganda.

"You should also leave now," Mehring advised me.

"For us it's different," I answered.

"We have to vote on Sunday," Carli added.

The coming Sunday was to be the day of Chancellor Schuschnigg's plebiscite. We, the people, were called upon to decide—yes or no, for or against a free, independent Austria. Sunday was also the thirteenth, but despite my superstitious mind, I never doubted the outcome. None of us did. A thundering "Yes" for our independence was predicted not only by Guido Zernatto, secretary general of the Fatherland Front and one of our authors, but also by Deputy Mayor Ernst Karl Winter, the main Socialist advocate of an anti-Nazi coalition and also Mehring's publisher. And German Ambassador Franz von Papen had confided to Alma Mahler Werfel that not even Nazis could officially call for Anschluss, since the Führer had received Schuschnigg at Berchtesgaden and signed a pledge to respect Austria's independence.

About the price of this pledge wild rumors flourished, but the published facts were depressing enough. Arthur von Seyss-Inquart, the Austrian government's official liaison with the Third Reich, would be made minister for state security; other Nazis would be put in key posts; amnesty would be given to those in jail, including the surviving killers of Schuschnigg's predecessor, Dr. Engelbert Dollfuss. . . .

I never forgot how the news about Chancellor Dollfuss's assassination had reached me in a summer resort, on July 25, 1934. Nazis had stormed into the Chancellery, shot him, and let the devout Catholic die on the floor of his office without even the last rites of his Church.

After Dollfuss's death Schuschnigg became our chancellor. Standing beside the bust of his murdered predecessor in the Vienna Parliament, Schuschnigg had recently declared: "This far and no farther." It was mid-February of 1938, just after he had made his "agreement" with Hitler at Berchtesgaden.

At the first word of Schuschnigg's trip to Berchtesgaden, I had made a horrified phone call to Guido Zernatto at Fatherland Front headquarters. "The chancellor went to Berchtesgaden? How could he?"

"That's what I asked him," replied the secretary general. On March 9, at Innsbruck in his native Tyrol, Schuschnigg announced the plebiscite for the thirteenth, giving us four days and Hitler no time to mount a counterattack. He closed with his vow of loyalty to the Austrian colors: *"Rot-weiss-rot bis in den Tod. . . ."*

"Red, white, and red to the death!" echoed his delirious audience. This had happened on Wednesday, two days before the three of us met at the Café Herrenhof, and we were still carried away. The killers were among us, but we were going to fight—and win! Not even Mehring would hear words of caution. Had not everyone in 1934 warned him against visiting the land of "Austro-fascism"? On the very train to Vienna a fellow passenger had told him of the Austrian ban on his new book. Then the gentleman had produced a copy and admiringly asked for an autograph.

"But—who are you?" Mehring had wanted to know.

"Well, I'm the censor. . . ."

Mehring never tired of telling the story, usually to prove his point that our situation was "hopeless but not serious," as the old Austrian joke from World War I days went. After a few jugs of new wine from the foothills of the Vienna Woods he sometimes called himself "a Viennese by choice."

In March, 1938, we even refused to be hopeless. We knew our choice: a free and independent Austria. We were convinced that Sunday would bring it into being. Mehring wanted to stay with us; if things went wrong after all, he said, he had friends at the Quai d'Orsay and might be able to help us get into France.

"Dr. Seyss-Inquart, please!" The waiter's voice broke into our conversation. "Dr. Seyss-Inquart—Berlin calling!"

A gentleman rose hastily at the next table. He had to squeeze past ours to get to the phone booth downstairs; for a moment I sat less than an arm's length from the new minister for state security. He was, it struck me for the first time, now in charge of our police!

On the shelf behind us stood a row of lovely bronze angels. When Seyss-Inquart emerged from the phone booth below us,

I pointed at them, whispering in Mehring's ear: "Should I drop one on his head?"

"Wouldn't help; too many left," he whispered back. He could not mean the angels. . . .

The minister for state security returned to his table, threw down a tip, and hurried out of the café. The waiter came to collect the tip. "Very nervous today, the Herr Doktor," he remarked to us, shaking his head. "Didn't even finish his apple strudel."

It was much later, in exile, that I learned from Guido Zernatto what the call from Berlin had been about. It sent Seyss-Inquart to the Federal Chancellery, where they had been looking high and low for him—in his department, at his law office, even at the formerly illegal Nazi-party headquarters on Seitzgasse—all in vain. Only his empty car had been found, parked in the Seitzgasse.

The desperate search was due to alarming reports that poured into the Chancellery. German troops were massing on the border and in Munich, the frontier town of Passau expected military convoys of some forty thousand men to arrive during the day, and in Lower Austria and in parts of Vienna itself S.A. and S.S. units were assembling with rucksacks. Seyss-Inquart, the government hoped, might ease the tension. Only the day before, on Thursday the tenth, he had agreed to make a broadcast for the plebiscite, and the belief in his loyalty died hard. That at the hour of greatest need for him he might be talking with Berlin at the Herrenhof—a well-chosen place, safe from eavesdroppers—was not suspected until he appeared at the Chancellery with his Nazi cabinet colleague, Minister without Portfolio Edmund Glaise-Horstenau.

The two gentlemen delivered an ultimatum. The Führer, they said, wished the plebiscite to be put off for a month and then to be conducted by Seyss-Inquart; should this be refused, they both would have to resign and to decline responsibility for the consequences. They gave the chancellor till 1 P.M. to decide—less than an hour.

6

Calling off the plebiscite seemed impossible for Schuschnigg. He said he could change the procedures but not the date, and he delegated Zernatto to seek an extension of the deadline from the two ministers while he himself would take up the situation with Federal President Wilhelm Miklas. Seyss-Inquart, after insisting that he had already stretched the time limit as far as he could, eventually consented to call Berlin once more and brought back a one-hour extension.

A silent crowd was waiting in the anteroom of the chancellor's office. The only sound was the constant ringing of telephones. Time passed—the last hour granted by Seyss-Inquart. Zernatto kept talking to him: These tactics, these policies so inconsistent with his every past stand—all this could not possibly be his own doing? The minister for state security admitted that it was not. Vienna, he said, was no longer the place for decisions. They would be made elsewhere.

"Where?"

"In Berlin."

"Or on the barricades," said Zernatto.

Seyss-Inquart thought this over and decided on another call to Marshal Hermann Göring, the man in charge in Berlin. This call was monitored in the Chancellery, and Seyss-Inquart's report on it proved wholly accurate. First, he said, Göring had kept him waiting on the line while he talked to the Führer; then the marshal had declared the ultimatum rejected, adding, "You tell that to Schuschnigg."

"Shall we convey the information to the chancellor?" Seyss-Inquart asked Zernatto.

"That," said the Austrian secretary of state, "is your personal job."

The minister for state security shrugged his shoulders. "I only carry the message," he said, "and no weight. I am nothing but a historic switchboard operator."

Austrian planes still circled overhead, showering Vienna with election-propaganda leaflets that fell unheeded in the midst of violent tumult. From the staid Café Herrenhof we went home through screaming street crowds. Only the Ballhausplatz, with the Chancellery, remained blocked off.

"Red, white, and red to the death!" rang from loudspeakers. "Heil Hitler!" the mobs yelled in between. I was whistling the "Marseillaise," but no one heard me. I felt far more militant than scared. Certain as ever of victory, Carli and I walked through jammed, riotous streets while Mehring tried to reach his hotel at the Westbahnhof, intending to pack his books, at least. The possibility of what was going on at the Chancellery during that hour never entered our minds.

Carli and I got safely to our "office," a room in my attic apartment in a villa in the neighborhood known as the Cottage. There the old streets were still calm, as if nothing had happened. The manuscripts of our authors lay peacefully piled on shelves. There were all shades of opinion there, with the sole exception of the Nazi shade. A reader for the Paul Zsolnay publishing house, its liaison with the Reich, had invited me to his home once and offered to get certain works such as mine admitted to the German market if our agency would take on a few Nazi spokesmen. We had refused, of course.

We were proud of our list—of Austrian clients like Franz Theodor Csokor, who had stood up at the last PEN Congress to cast Austria's vote against permitting Nazis in that literary world organization; of the essays we got from Thomas Mann and other famous refugees from Hitler, like Essad Bey, a Moslem, today much discussed in America as author of the revived pseudonymous novel *Ali and Nino*. We also handled foreign rights such as the ones to *Three Times Austria*, Kurt von Schuschnigg's own rebuttal of the anschluss propagandists. We spent that Friday afternoon working as usual; keeping cool seemed more important than anything else. When we were through, I went to visit my father, then living with my young stepmother near his Biochemical Institute. My mother, a feminist and pacifist, as I was, had died long before.

From the streetcar, which followed a route outside the

8

center of the city, things looked quieter. I found my father depressed, my stepmother combative. We kept the radio on, and shortly after seven we heard our chancellor report to the Austrian people:

"This day has confronted us with a difficult and critical situation," he began. "The government of the German Reich has presented to the Federal President an ultimatum with a time limit, demanding the formation of a government according to German proposals, with the entrance of German troops into Austria at this hour to be envisioned otherwise. I state before the world that the reports disseminated throughout Austria to the effect that rivers of blood have been shed, that the government has lost control of the situation and could not have restored order on its own, are inventions from A to Z."

I breathed easier.

"The Federal President has instructed me to inform the Austrian people that we are yielding to force. Determined at all costs and even in this grave hour to avoid shedding German blood, we have instructed our armed forces to withdraw without resistance."

My non-German blood boiled in my ears. All I could hear of the rest was the closing sentence.

"And so, in this hour, I take my leave of the Austrian people with the heartfelt wish: God save Austria."

"Oh, my God," said my stepmother.

Music followed, a familiar tune by Joseph Haydn which had been used in Hapsburg days as our national hymn. My father seemed relieved all of a sudden. "It can't be quite that bad," he said, "if they're playing the old imperial anthem."

I stared at him. Had it not been a weeping matter, I would have laughed, but no tears came either. To my generation, grown up after World War I, the tune we heard no longer recalled the old monarchy. The text that we connected with the ancient melody was a less reassuring one: "Deutschland über Alles."

Germany above all else—above all else in the world. . . .

9

I sat staring into the void. And from the void, rejoicing burst in: "March, and don't spare a windowpane till the last rock's been hurled"—the music was new, the idea expanded—"Germany we own today; tomorrow we'll own the world!"

I wanted out, away from here—where to? *"Auf Wiedersehen,"* I said mechanically. *"Auf Wiedersehen* across the border."

"For God's sake," Papa hissed, closing the window. "What if someone hears you? I'm staying."

And as though in protest, my youthful stepmother cried, "Think of us when you're at the border!" Eventually, as it turned out, he would leave—and she would stay. . . .

Nothing made sense any more. I still thought of warning my father to get his things from the institute, where they were sure to be confiscated. I knew his sacred instruments, the golden balances that allowed him to weigh milligrams of tissue. "From my institute?" he repeated incredulously. It was his world. He looked lost at the idea that evidently struck him now for the first time: He would have to give up his cancer research.

The lost look ushered me into the street, among voices bellowing out of the dark: "One folk, one Reich, one Führer!" Faceless voices ringed me, and there were no barricades to hold them off. I pressed myself into a phone booth, got my connection: "Come straight to my place," I told Walter Mehring.

"Yes." Click. The connection was broken. I felt all alone. Had Walter hung up? In my ears his voice went on: "May God answer our plea and never loose the Great Cancer. . . ." The words came from a ballad he had written years back about a monster locked in the zodiac or in the depths of a bottomless German lake. It was not the cancer my father would have to stop fighting; it was a worse one that had got loose and was approaching me now step by step, as in Mehring's poem: "When from its dream the fuddled creature wakes, it's backward and awry for all—backward and awry to

10

pogrom and auto-da-fé. . . ." Yes, that was how it went on. Suddenly the Cancer had faces, the many faces of the "folk comrades" who were all around, chanting, dancing for joy. "With Jew blood spurting from the blade, a knife cuts twice as well," they sang to the tune of their glorified pimp, Horst Wessel.

I felt I was running, running faster than I had at noon to the Herrenhof, with the Great Cancer hard on my heels. "And backward runs the century clock / Strikes midnight for eternity."

Bells tolled: God save Austria. . . . God save us all. . . .

I ran up three flights of stairs and slammed a door. I was home, or at least in what would be home till tomorrow. Manuscripts covered the floor; a familiar face looked up. All was quiet. Carli got up to embrace me like an escapee from hell.

"Just so you're here," he said.

I asked what he was doing.

"Packing manuscripts."

I shrugged. "Why bother? We can't take them with us."

"We've got to get rid of them," he said—of the dangerous ones, at least. We had no stove, only gas heat, so we could not burn them; he wanted to drop them in the shrubbery behind the fences of gardens along our street.

"Don't leave me alone now, please," I begged, adding that Mehring would come any minute; then he could perform his errand. Carli stayed.

It was past nine when Mehring arrived, his face ashen. Bands of rioters had stopped his cab; the driver had managed to lose them by speeding through dark alleys. "Swine," the man had muttered and volunteered the latest information: The inner city was cordoned off, the Chancellery seized by the S.S., Schuschnigg arrested. Mehring hardly took the time to get out of his overcoat before picking up the phone. "You want to call someone?" I asked.

"Paris. Quai d'Orsay."

All night, from my phone, he kept trying to reach the French Foreign Ministry—as if his friends there could help. It did not occur to us that we were asking for trouble. All we knew was that the call did not go through.

All night we unwittingly tried senseless expedients, perhaps simply because life had ceased to make sense. All night Carli tramped the streets with anti-Nazi material under his arm, just to get it out of my apartment. About midnight, a news flash said that "Federal Chancellor Seyss-Inquart" had asked Berlin to dispatch German troops to Austria. We refused to believe it and started telephoning all over Vienna during the first hours of Saturday, March 12. Zernatto's number did not answer; we concluded that he must be under arrest. But we went right on calling others.

Csokor answered. "Pack," he said. "See you later." He hung up.

We sat paralyzed among our remaining manuscripts. Mehring did not dare set foot in his hotel again; at dawn Carli went instead to fetch him the essentials and returned with a small suitcase and the news that the Gestapo had been looking for Mehring at 2 A.M. Not where he really was, thank heaven.

By way of a good-morning greeting the radio blared an announcement: "The requested German units have now crossed the border. Reichsführer of S.S. Himmler has arrived at the Hotel Imperial. The Führer himself is en route to Vienna. *Sieg Heil!*"

When would they get to us? We stole out of the house and down the empty tree-lined streets of old villas. Thunder filled the sky as flight after flight of swastika-winged planes roared overhead, so many that they obscured the rising sun.

We found a dark corner in a little café. The waiter brought two newspapers, one of them long known as a Nazi organ. The rest, he said, had been seized because the Germans were coming.

12

Mehring ordered cognac rather than coffee. The waiter showed no surprise. "Walter," I said, "we'll have to put you on the next train." He ordered another cognac. Carli and I had black coffee. We paid and left.

On the way to the station Carli said each of us should travel alone, in the order of peril: "Mehring, you first, then Hertha, then I." There were no objections. Misery loves company, but this time safety did not lie in numbers.

Black uniforms around the main gate at the Westbahnhof caught our eyes a block away. Mehring turned back. "I can't."

We walked in circles, almost blundering too close to his hotel. I urged him not to miss the daytime express to Paris; it was due to leave soon. A hopeless shrug answered.

"We'll be waiting for word at my place," I kept insisting. "If your wire from Zurich doesn't come tonight, we'll start looking for you. We'll leave nothing undone; you know that. We'll get help somewhere—and as soon as it comes, we'll follow. . . ."

"What should I wire?" he murmured. It had to be simple but singular, meaningless but not so meaningless as to suggest a code. We agreed on "Greetings, Uncle Emil."

Through an unguarded side entrance we finally slipped into the terminal, and Carli went to the ticket window while I stood chatting with Mehring—in French, because in lieu of passport he carried a French travel pass. On Track 1 the train was waiting.

"Vienna-Zurich-Paris Express—all aboard," the conductor called just as Carli brought the ticket and the little suitcase. Mehring set out for the train. Then an S.S. man came over, and Mehring's filigree figure all but faded in the shadow of the black uniform.

"Who's that?" The enemy pointed at the shrinking poet.

Carli stepped in. "Our French teacher," he said quickly and drew out his student card as if to offer it in evidence.

"Yes, our French teacher," I echoed from the other side.

The S.S. man's attention shifted to us. While the student card underwent his malevolent scrutiny, I heard a sound and glanced sideways: Mehring seemed to have vanished. The train whistle blew. A slight figure climbed onto the platform of the last car.

"Stop!" someone shouted.

We froze. Then we saw S.S. men converge on a group of four or five people still heading for the train. Carli was right: Groups were riskier. The four or five were surrounded and taken away as the train pulled out slowly and the rumbling wheels blended into the roar of the bombers circling above.

From my house, to which we returned with some difficulty, a swastika flag waved to greet us. I knocked at the door of my landlady's apartment on the second floor. A distraught Frau Kornfeld opened and sighed with relief to see no one but us.

"What's the idea, Malvina?" I bristled. "Where did you get that rag?"

She was still shaking. "They brought them around—every house must have one——"

"Take the swastika down, or you're going to see what'll happen," I screamed, beside myself. Actually, I did not know what I could do about it. We left Malvina standing in the door, went upstairs, and watched through the dormer window as the loathsome flag disappeared.

It had not been gone five minutes when Malvina came panting up with tears in her eyes. "Thank you, Hertherl, thank you," she sobbed. "The radio just said Jews are not allowed to fly the swastika—if they do, they'll be arrested. You've saved our lives."

There she was unfortunately mistaken. In the long run the flag incident made no difference: Herr and Frau Kornfeld both ended in Auschwitz. "No matter, the Jew must burn," as a great German writer of the enlightened eighteenth century sardonically put it.

14

When I saw Malvina later on that Saturday afternoon, I took pains not to let her suspect that it might be for the last time. "Listen: We're going away just for the weekend," I said, impressing it upon her. "If anyone should ask, I'll be back Monday."

She nodded. "See you Monday, Hertherl"—but tears were in her eyes again. It was our farewell.

In the evening there were knocks on my door. Carli and I ran to open it, but it was not the expected telegram. It was one of our favorite authors, Franz Theodor Csokor, keeping his promise, with a much younger colleague and friend, Odon von Horvath. They had lately become as inseparable as Castor and Pollux. And Csokor used to remark that when Odon came into the room, I saw nobody but him.

I had also known Odon for a long time; we had met in Berlin after the opening of his *Tales from the Vienna Woods* in 1931. The play, in which I, just a beginner, had only a walk-on role, won him a Kleist Prize, Germany's most prestigious drama award; but when I congratulated him on the rave notices he had received, he broke into a grin: "Wait till you see the pannings. I'll show you those tomorrow."

And he did. "They're mad at me," he stated, beaming. His play not only showed up the proverbial Viennese *Gemütlichkeit* but also it paraded fullfledged Nazis over the stage two years before they took over. "Aren't they beastly?" Odon would comment with relish.

It was his favorite phrase. Even now, with the Nazis on the rampage in Vienna, he arrived asking, "Aren't they beastly?" He looked calm and phlegmatic as ever, even though temporarily without relish. "Csok," he said, musing, "you could stay here, couldn't you? You wouldn't have to get out."

The Austrian poet laureate shook his graying lion's mane. "No, I wouldn't—not if I denounced our PEN resolution. But I'm not the Führer," he chuckled. "My signatures stand." In the morning he planned to depart for Poland, where his

translations of many Polish classics had earned him a medal
and a standing governmental invitation.

"You're right," Odon agreed. "The main thing is to keep
working. We'll have to become more self-centered to be less
selfish." His own plan was to go briefly to friends in Czechoslovakia and then to Amsterdam, where a German emigré
publisher was bringing out his novels—*The Age of the Fish*,
which later appeared in America, and *A Child of Our Time*,
about a Nazi soldier who starts to think and goes on to
speak to us beyond his death.

All night he and Csokor stayed with Carli and me,
waiting for word from "Uncle Emil" and discussing escape
chances, both ours and our friends'. His great colleague
Franz Werfel was safe in Italy, but Werfel's wife, Alma, was
still in town with Anna, her daughter by Gustav Mahler,
the late composer; they too would leave for Czechoslovakia
in the morning. Several others we knew about wanted to
try that closest, though presumably most closely watched,
of the saving frontiers.

"When shall we four meet again?" I paraphrased Macbeth,
opening not a witches' cauldron but my last bottle of wine
from the Vienna Woods. Behind drawn curtains, by dim
light, we sat there clinking glasses until the bottle was
empty and the new dawn graying outside.

No telegram had come, and we no longer talked of anything but poor Mehring. Conspiratorial plans were laid and
discarded. Try to notify his Parisian friends? Impossible. Have
someone check with the Gestapo? Whom? Baron Horvath,
Odon's father, headed the Danube Steamship Company in
Munich and had all kinds of connections. It gave me an idea:
Perhaps we should leave via Munich?

Carli stomped his foot. "You can't! That's insane!"

"Calm down, children," Csokor growled.

We continued in whispers. How about Von Papen? He
had a heart for poets and a weakness for the Werfels. . . .
"Let's see Alma," Horvath decided. "She's a woman who
knows how to get what she wants. Come on, Csok."

16

They set out at once. *"Auf Wiedersehen,"* we all said—but we four were never to meet again.

Daylight filtered through the blinds. Carli turned on the radio; the excited announcer could hardly keep up with all the good news. "Mussolini will give the Führer the South Tyrol as Austria's dowry at her union with the Reich—*Sieg Heil!* . . . Our Cardinal Innitzer has sent the Führer a telegram of welcome—*Sieg Heil!"*

Church bells tolled. It was Sunday. We turned off the radio and waited silently, endlessly. Someone heavy-booted came up the stairs, knocked on my door—Gestapo? Carli went to open it.

"Fräulein Pauli?" The postal messenger held out a telegram. I signed for it, and after closing the door, we read and reread the message, though all it said was what we had agreed upon: "GREETINGS, UNCLE EMIL."

We started packing my things, but our minds were far away in Switzerland. Was Mehring still there? The telegram had been filed in Zurich some ten hours after the scheduled arrival of his train. What had happened at the border?

"I'll soon find out," I said.

"How about me?" Carli sounded impatient and a bit resentful that his own plan obliged him to stay behind once more. We agreed on another telegram, which I would send from Zurich, unsigned: "Manuscript arrived, send copy."

We were about to go downstairs when the phone rang. It was the last call that reached us: "Alma wasn't there any more," Csokor said.

"I'm on my way to Uncle Emil," I answered.

"Thank God," I heard. *"Auf Wiedersehen."* Click.

Auf Wiedersehen—if ever. . . .

A human tide engulfed us on the way to the Westbahnhof. Were they in flight, or were they going there to hail the arriving Führer? The station was full of German troops and S.S., and loudspeakers brayed their triumph from the roof. The wait in line before the ticket window seemed interminable, but at last I managed to buy a round-trip Vienna-Paris-

Vienna ticket that would lend a harmless coloring to my departure. Besides, in Paris an unused return ticket could be exchanged for a cash refund that would be most helpful, for the amount one was allowed to take across the frontier was only ten Austrian schillings—about three dollars.

At the gate to the tracks two S.S. men strode up and down, up and down; the black uniforms also went in pairs. Who's afraid of the big black wolf? Whistling inaudibly through clenched teeth, I walked up to the nearest one. "Now that the border is open, can one go to Munich without a visa?"

He looked me over. "Just go ahead; and you'll find out," he snarled, but he let me pass and did not even watch which track I was heading for. Only Carli followed me with his eyes as I boarded a crowded express for Zurich and Paris which should have left hours earlier.

I managed to find a seat in one compartment. Thank God I met no one I knew, no one to ask questions. I left my suitcase on the seat and returned to the aisle to look once more for Carli; he was standing far back on the platform. Our eyes met, but he did not dare wave; he only raised his hand a little when the train pulled out at last, late in the day. Sunday the thirteenth, the day that should have brought us victory at the polls, was nearly over.

In my compartment nobody said a word. The conductor came to punch the tickets as usual. A shadowy, familiar landscape passed outside as we rolled into the night. I felt incredibly exhausted, like a boxer after a knockout. Red, white, and red to the death. . . . My eyes closed; I was so tired. I think I wished I was dead.

Now and then I came to and looked out. We stopped in Salzburg, the festival town. Only last summer all of us had been there for Max Reinhardt's last performance of *Everyman*—Csokor, Horvath, Mehring, the Werfels, Carli, and I. Then the train rolled on. At Innsbruck a man came into our car, a man with a tanned face I knew from pictures: It must be Hannes Schneider, whose name was a synonym for skiing in Austria. Last month, on the day of Schuschnigg's trip to Berchtesgaden, Carli and I had put on skis for the last time. How long ago it seemed. . . . The ski champion stood in the aisle, looking out the window, watching the telegraph poles rush by. Another day dawned; we were hours behind schedule. The mountains gleamed white, cut into slices by the telegraph poles. More and more patches of snow accompanied us as we climbed out of the valley toward the Arlberg, where Schneider had his home.

At the last stop before the long tunnel a Nazi horde suddenly stormed the train—teen-agers in Tyrolean leather pants, wearing swastika arm bands, swaggering, bullying, sniffing around the compartments. "Why aren't you in school?" I asked them when they came to me.

For a moment they seemed nonplussed; then they broke into embarrassed grins. "Doesn't make sense any more," one said. "We just got out of jail. Now we run the other fellows in." They all spoke the local dialect.

"Won't be long till there's war, anyway," another said, beaming.

I nodded. "Good for you," I said and showed them my open suitcase. There were some chocolate bars that Carli had thought of packing for me; I took them out. "Here, you'll like these."

"We can't take anything," one said longingly.

"It isn't anything," I said. "Just chocolate." They took the bars and left for the next compartment, chewing their candy and ducking respectfully past Hannes Schneider in the aisle. Him they knew.

At Feldkirch, the border station, the train jolted to a stop. S.S. men came aboard instead of Austrian customs officials, and everyone in our compartment paled at the sight of the black uniforms. Doors were locked, passports collected, names checked against lists, and all suitcases opened, the contents dumped on the floor and ransacked. Several passengers

19

had to take off their shoes and watch the soles being slit with knives. Some of them were hauled into the aisles and led away.

An empty seat next to me was promptly occupied by a black uniform. It was my turn. Don't hem and haw, I warned myself; brazen it out. . . . "Why did you leave from the Westbahnhof?"

Idiotic question. "That's where trains for Paris leave," I answered, showing my ticket. "Here—I'll be back in a week."

He studied it. "What do you want in Paris?"

"To sell German books to French publishers."

"Why just now?"

"I have put it off twice," I replied. "Now I have to go."

The cross-examination went in circles—why, where from, where to, how, with whom, what for. I felt the noose tighten round my neck until I could hardly breathe. The S.S. man's eyes almost drove me out of my mind; I stared back. They were gray-greenish werewolf's eyes that never left mine, and my right index and middle fingers began to stiffen and spread by themselves into a V shape. Got to beat him to it, I told myself, to catch him off balance—fingers stiff, the right distance apart, and then a quick, hard stab at both eyes, as far in as I can go. . . .

His was the only uniform I saw; perhaps his fellows were busy elsewhere. He kept asking, and I kept answering, I did not know what. I never moved, never took my eyes off his. . . . "Why did you leave last night?"

The circle started all over again—why this, why that. The eyes that I must not miss seemed to be going round and round. "Why particularly *last* night?"

"I wanted to wait for the Führer's arrival."

I felt passengers edge away from me. The black one leaned forward. Slowly, imperceptibly, my hand moved up, aiming two V-spread fingers.

He blinked. All of a sudden my fingers held a passport. My passport.

20

That was close, I thought as he turned away and began to slash the upholstery, looking for valuables. I had none; I had nothing to lose. Those who had something were taken off the train. After more than five hours the S.S. withdrew, barking "Heil Hitler."

Our compartment looked like a junkyard by the time the train started moving. Some seats stayed empty. In the aisle Hannes Schneider was standing, looking out the window again, and there could be no doubt: He was coming with us.

The wheels rumbled. Outside someone whistled, waving a flag. Instead of the swastika, it showed a peaceful white cross on a red ground. We must have crossed the border. We were in Switzerland.

CHAPTER 2

The Little Hotels

Look not behind thee. . . . The biblical injunction for the flight from Sodom seemed addressed to me now. Nightmares haunted my first hours of safe sleep in Zurich. I dreamed I was looking for a way back and running in circles, round and round, until my limbs froze.

In the morning I heard at the Café Odeon that another Austrian refugee had jumped out of her hotel-room window that night. Killed instantly. Nobody knew who she was. I squeezed into a corner as if to duck strange questions and strange eyes. Yesterday I had sent Carli a wire with my hotel address; if it reached him promptly, he could be with me tonight. I'd have to wait. Mehring was no longer in Zurich. As agreed, he left word for me at the Oprecht publishing offices, near the Odeon: I'd have to hurry; the French border too might be closed at any moment. He had scrawled the note in haste, adding his hotel address in Paris.

The secretary at Oprecht's echoed the warning. She had some money for me; we had just sold them a book of Mehring's. Dr. and Mrs. Oprecht were in conference right now—could I come back later, perhaps? Perhaps. . . . (Later the Oprechts helped to draw up lists and to raise funds for the rescue of anti-Nazi writers.)

At the moment I had no one else to turn to in Zurich. My brother Wolfgang lived there—he was a professor at the Poly, as the Swiss call their Federal Institute of Technology— but he just happened to be in England, lecturing. I was alone at the café, waiting, scarcely daring to move. A small corner of the lake peered through the windows, with white swans circling elegantly past the children, who threw them bread crumbs. A picture of peace.

The sun rose higher; the smoke clouds in the café were dancing in the rays that led to stacks of newspapers strewn over a long table—all the world's news in piles. The same headline jumped at me in many languages: "HITLER IN VIENNA." I went over and brought back a couple of papers to my corner. The letters danced before my eyes like spots in the sunlight. They formed a picture: the Führer in his big black Mercedes, riding along the Ringstrasse between swastika flags and waving crowds. . . . I shut my eyes. The harsh voice of the Führer pursued me in the darkness: "I now make before history the greatest report of my life: Austria has come home to the Reich."

Home. Where was mine? "The greatest report of my life"—I'll never get over that. I did not notice the tears in my eyes till a creaking sound made me look up and I had trouble seeing the figure that came through the revolving door. The tears were running down my cheeks. "Carli," I called. It was impossible. "Carli."

Heads turned; eyes peered curiously out of the clouds of blue smoke. It did not matter. Carli put down a suitcase and came to me. He had come straight from the station to the café.

"What made you think I'd be here?"

"I don't know," he said.

My telegram . . . ?

"I couldn't wait." A man with a swastika in his lapel had been tailing him as he returned form the Vienna West-bahnhof. When Carli stopped to face him, the pursuer turned out to be one of our authors. "You're being watched. Come along," he whispered, taking Carli's arm and leading him down a side street. "Where is Fräulein Pauli?"

Carli shrugged. The Nazi understood. "Take the next train out," he urged, waving up a taxi. "You want to pack? I'll come with you. Where to?"

As though under compulsion, Carli gave his home address. While he was upstairs, the man he could not shake stood waiting in the street; the phrase "protective custody" ran through Carli's mind when they were back in the cab and bound for the terminal again, Carli now with a suitcase. "We'll get back to normal soon; then you can come back with Fräulein Pauli," his escort assured him as he boarded the train. "Tell her that I accompanied you in the streets" was the last thing Carli heard from the platform.

I shrugged; gangsters don't get back to normal. But we were together again, Carli and I. He asked about Walter, and I showed him the note. "He's right," Carli said. "Let's get going."

He looked exhausted. We ordered coffee and something to eat while comparing experiences. What killed so many others had saved Carli: He took too much money along, and when the Nazi teen-agers burst in at Feldkirch, he just held out schilling notes to them. "Confiscated," they announced, took the money, and left him in peace.

"Where do you think you're going?" an S.S. man asked on the platform in Feldkirch.

"To the luggage counter, for my skis," Carli replied.

He called a porter, and in handing over his suitcase, slipped the man the permissible ten schillings. The old porter grinned and led the way past the luggage counter, through a luggage car, through freight cars, and across dead-end tracks, Carli hard on his heels. Somehow, evidently, they got through the barrier and on another train. Carli's suitcase was in his hand; the old man had vanished.

"An Austrian miracle," I said.

Carli shook his head. "Good old Austrian inefficiency."

We laughed, paid our bill with the Oprecht money, and left the café. From my hotel we went to the station and wired news of our arrival to Mehring in Paris. Habits form fast: Before getting on the Basel-Paris express, we looked right and left for pursuers, but here there were none.

At the French frontier our Austrian passports were stamped as if everything were in perfect order. We could breathe easier. The train was so empty we could even lie down and doze all the way to Paris. At the Gare de l'Est, beret pulled over his forehead, stood Walter Mehring, waiting.

He drew us aside like conspirators. "I called my friend Comert at the Quai d'Orsay," he began, as though resuming our last talk in Vienna, "and had the border reopened for you for one hour."

At first we regarded this as one of his poetic fancies, the sort of joke we called meringues. It turned out, however, that the French-Swiss border actually had been closed earlier and then very briefly reopened.

We were no longer surprised at anything. Mehring's account of his own escape was dramatic: Hauled off the train with other suspects and ordered through a door to the right, he had had the presence of mind to slip through another door, to the left. . . . Just like that, I thought, remembering our night of worry about the Gestapo lists his name must be on.

He spoke only French now. He brought us to his hotel, where he had reserved rooms for us—the cheapest in the house but with all the necessities: bed, closet, table, chair.

For the bathroom you had to go across the courtyard. The front entrance of the Hôtel de l'Univers opened on the narrow, dirty Rue Monsieur le Prince, a side street off the Boulevard Saint-Michel, a step from the Luxembourg Gardens and not far from the Sorbonne.

Our first walk took us down the "Boul' Mich" to the Île de la Cité and into the iron-gray complex of the Palais de Justice, where kings had dwelt once and where we had now to report to police headquarters. Our Austrian passports were still valid, so the prefecture gave each of us a *permis de séjour*, a short-term permit to stay, which did not, of course, confer any right to work. For the prerogatives of normal foreign residents of France, entitled to hold regular *cartes d'identité* such as the one Mehring, for instance, still possessed from years past—for those we were definitely not *en règle*.

Later on the same day, Mehring had made an appointment for me and himself with his friend Pierre Comert, minister plenipotentiary in charge of press relations. The stylish gentleman with the neat moustache received us cordially in his office at the Quai d'Orsay; he was glad we had hurried, for now one required a visa to enter from Switzerland. My thanks were waved aside: *"Pas de quoi, madame"*—"Don't mention it."

I felt encouraged to speak of the horrors in Austria, but there I was interrupted. One had direct reports; at least the union with Germany had been accomplished without force of arms, indeed quite peaceably. "You can see in the newsreels how enthusiastically Monsieur Hitler was welcomed."

Nonenthusiasts were neither seen nor heard of. Schuschnigg, I learned, was "confined to his home" and "well treated"—that the treatment included Gestapo refinements like keeping you awake all night was not then suspected at the French Foreign Office. To me only one thing was new: Wilhelm Miklas, the formal Federal President of Austria, had steadfastly refused to name Seyss-Inquart chancellor and

27

to sign the Anschluss law. I heard that this, of course, did cast some doubt on the legality of the proceeding and thus on the prospects of its recognition by France.

"Miklas firm," said the official report. The news from Berlin was that instead of ranting, Göring had decided to laugh it off: "A man with fourteen children knows how to be firm," M. Comert said with a smile that made me wonder whether the words were his or Göring's. Miklas had simply gone home. There were no reports of anything untoward having happened to him.

I should have stayed on, it ran through my mind; resistance does impress them. As far as I was concerned, Comert told me, I could not take a job, but he assured me that I could write, publish, even carry on my agency. Should I have other desires, he would be glad to see me any time. A courteous gesture closed the interview.

"Peace—it's wonderful. Do you believe what he says?" I asked Mehring outside.

"Maybe just a meringue." He smiled as he lit a cigarette. "An atrocity story. . . ."

Harmoniously we wandered back to our little hotel, he to his accustomed routine, which he had broken only this once, for my sake. Wherever he was, in Berlin or Vienna or later on both shores of America, he would rise early, take a short walk—in Paris to the Luxembourg—and then start working. On the wobbly table of his hotel room, dipping an old pen in blue ink, he wrote line after slightly rising line on loose sheets of paper. The lines formed themselves into poems, and the poems in their rhythmic ups and downs followed the drift of our lives: "Dumped by the railway into swirling valleys of massed mankind, you drift—convulsed by spells of phthisis of the wallet—through the alleys that shrink and bend and shrink and end at the little hotels. . . ."

Ours was an old, respectable hotel, by no means a house of ill fame, as some would have it later; true, next door we had one such, marked by an inviting blinker light. Our Univers was always in darkness, notably so the back rooms like my ground-floor one that opened on the walled-in courtyard. Except for the kittens that used to play there, the courtyard made one think of a jail.

Though free, Carli and I had neither work nor leisure. We drifted through the narrow streets and alleys of the Latin Quarter, which was full of our predecessors, the anti-Nazi German refugees who had been around for years. I knew and loved Paris from previous visits; recently I had worked there in a picture for Paramount. Now the newsreels were showing the latest pictures from Vienna, the broad, endless river of the Nazi columns, and when we came out of the theater, the *Ville Lumière* seemed changed and dark. The alleys pushed us between steeply shrinking walls as we walked on from the Rue Monsieur le Prince over to the Rue du Chat Qui Pêche. Each Parisian *quartier* seemed like a separate village along the Seine River. There were Frenchmen who not only never left the country but hardly ever left their districts. Even M. and Mme. Boucher, the proprietors of the Hôtel de l'Univers, sometimes gave this impression.

Not even the longest *métro* ride brought you close to nature. There were only the parks, large and small, nearby and far away—but however well kept their lawns, however beautiful their old trees, we still missed the Vienna Woods. Probably we found Paris changed because it did not offer us a way out; that we ourselves had changed did not occur to us.

In the Luxembourg Gardens the trees were in bloom. The air smelled faintly of spring. We would sit on a bench, Carli and I, and watch the children sail their boats on the small pond till one of the toys got out of reach or capsized. The children cried then. We could not help. We too felt as if we had been shipwrecked.

The trees rustled and the pond cast tiny waves; I felt a touch of wanderlust. There was no road back—only forward. When would we get across the Big Pond? America had long been in my dreams; many of my former stage colleagues

—the actors Peter Lorre and Franz Lederer and even the famous director Max Reinhardt—were already in Hollywood. Before long, Carli and I were headed for the U. S. Consulate to find out what could be done to get a visa.

The fountain in the Place de la Concorde shot glittering loops into the sunlight. On the far side of it, near the Hôtel Crillon, we could see the tail end of a line of people stretching from the Rue Royale around the corner to our objective. Evidently our notion of reaching America was unoriginal as well as unpromising. To make quite sure, we joined the line anyway, patiently inching along with it to the information window of the Consulate.

The information was depressing. The immigration quotas were filled for decades to come, and visitor's visas were issued only to persons able to return to their countries of origin. That left us out.

Que faire? Ahead of us the broad Champs-Élysées stretched to the Arch of Triumph. "Let's play tourists," Carli proposed.

It was all right with me. Tourists in Paris climb the Arc de Triomphe to get a bird's-eye view of the radiant metropolis, and so we strolled up the Champs-Élysées. This was an upper-class neighborhood, better situated, with many Russian emigrés, and the small tables so cheerfully set on the sidewalk before the cafés attracted others who had arrived, many from the international world of films. Later we learned how to play along there too; at the time we were just playing tourists. It was fun, in a way, but not as much fun as it used to be.

Before the Tomb of the Unknown Soldier we halted. There are unknown soldiers everywhere, and we silently greeted this one before climbing the stairs into the focus of the star formed by the great boulevards meeting from every direction, filled with surging humanity and chrome-flashing columns of autos.

The view darkened. It might be only a cloud crossing the sky, but to me the roar of Parisian traffic seemed to swell menacingly and the shadows to assume eerie dimensions. These were not cloud shadows. . . . Once again I saw and heard the Luftwaffe thunder across a blue sky. "March, march!" it bellowed in my ears. "Germany we've got today; tomorrow we'll have the world!" I saw swastika flags over a river of flashing steel helmets. I saw them goose-step up the Champs-Élysées as on the Ring in Vienna.

I felt dizzy on the Arch of Triumph. "They're coming— the Germans are coming," I cried, grabbing Carli's arm. He stared at me uncomprehendingly while in my mind the black columns kept drawing nearer, nearer to the crumbling star of streets under our feet.

It was like a mirror image of Vienna, that vision of the Nazi victory parade on the Champs-Élysées, and before I recovered—that day or the next, certainly before the end of our first week in Paris—a swastika sought me out in our little hotel. It adorned a letter that Mme. Boucher handed me from her concierge's box. I turned pale and did not dare open it until I was in my room. The swastika was an official stamp, but the letter was postmarked Paris. It came not from the Reich but from the German Consulate General. My God, what did they want of me? I ripped the envelope open. A ballot form fell out:

Do you agree to AUSTRIA'S REUNION WITH THE GERMAN REICH as accomplished on March 13, and do you vote for the list of our Führer ADOLF HITLER?

Printed underneath the question were a large circle for a "yes" vote and a small one for a possible "no." An enclosed circular informed me that the plebiscite in Austria was scheduled for April 10, that buses would be running from the Consulate General in Paris to the nearest polling place across the border, and that for every German from

Austria participation was a patriotic duty. "Register to vote! Heil Hitler! "

I burst out laughing wildly. So this was the way back they had in mind. I gave a start when the door opened—had someone heard me laugh? It was only Carli. I drew him in and locked the door before showing him the piece of paper. Had he received one too? He shook his head. I paced up and down as in a cell. "Where did they get my address? Where?"

I had no contact with anyone across the border, not even with my father. Could there be a spy in our group? I thought of the Café de Tournon next door, where Joseph Roth, the journalist and novelist, held court; among the habitués at his table were not only well-known literary fugitives but also odd "political" types such as Hermann Rauschning, the former Nazi president of the Danzig Senate. I sought to avoid him whenever possible, even though Roth assured me he was now giving vital information to the British government. Perhaps he gave other information elsewhere?

Carli did not share my suspicions. After all, our addresses were on file at the Prefecture; no doubt the French had given them to official representatives of a foreign power. It sounded plausible. But why no summons for Carli? Surely Jews couldn't vote, he replied.

"We'd rather be the playmates of hyenas than howl with the 'folk comrades' over there," I quoted from Mehring's "Emigrants' Song," our new national anthem: "All that was home once and the bit of fatherland, that's what the emigrant carries in his bandanna, on his soles, to every man and land between the poles. . . ." It was one more item for the bandanna—my "patriotic duty," this new greeting from home.

In the evening I showed the ballot to Joseph Roth at his round corner table opposite the bar, with its battery of bottles, where he sat hunched over a sheet of paper and a water glass as usual. You had to look closely to note that the glass held slivovitz.

The Little Hotels

A sip punctuated each sentence the writer put down; the glass would empty slowly and surely as the paper filled up with his dainty, meticulous script. He worked like this all day and most of the night. The book he had just finished, *Die Kapuzinergruft*—the crypt of the Capuchins in Vienna is the Hapsburgs' burial place—was a sequel to his *Radetzky March*, the great Austrian novel of the decade. In his books Roth carried on the same tradition as in his manners, in his posture, in his casual reminders that he had been an Imperial and Royal officer in World War I. I knew him from his visits to Vienna, though from the early twenties on he had lived in Frankfurt and since 1933 had been living in Paris.

He always got up ceremoniously when a lady approached; the unsteadiness was all but imperceptible. He kissed your hand, bowing so low that on the back of it you felt his blond moustache, damp and bristly. Then the hazy blue eyes wandered off as a gesture invited you to the table. Never missing were Roth's boyhood friend, novelist Soma Morgenstern, who came from the same Galician-Jewish background Roth did, and the lovely dark-skinned Manga Bell, who was like a shadow accompanying Roth in exile. She was married to a king or chieftain from French Cameroun, and people told each other that the king was still waiting for her and that Cameroun subjects would fall on their knees if they chanced to meet her in Paris.

To me these stories always seemed too much like fairy tales—until thirty years later, in the Swiss canton of Ticino, I happened to fall into conversation with two exchange students from the Republic of Cameroun. When I mentioned my old friend Manga, the young Africans' expressions changed abruptly from polite detachment to wondering awe. "*La femme du chef,*" one said.

"*Du roi,*" the other corrected him. "You really knew Manga Bell?"

I described the slim beauty with the olive skin. We had lost sight of her when Paris fell; now I heard that even in

33

Cameroun nobody knew what had become of her. Her husband, after the French collapse, had been the first African ruler to join Charles de Gaulle's Free French and to keep on fighting Hitler. Later he himself had died a mysterious death. At the Italian frontier post I left the two students. Our ways parted; they shook my hand, and I saw their eyes follow me as I drove on—someone who had known their queen. . . .

At Roth's table Manga was quite simply one of us. She alone could have gone back to her country, but she preferred to stay with Roth and us. The red rose he presented her with each morning, fresh, used to be her only adornment. It remained on her shoulder, slowly wilting away.

Roth, who hardly ever left his table, was in touch with God and the world, as the German saying goes. He always knew what went on behind the scenes; his correspondents ranged from Thomas Mann, in the United States, to Otto von Hapsburg, then an exile in Belgium. Late at night he liked to call himself a monarchist, and none of his friends from left to right would take offense or even take it seriously. We did not know where Roth really stood. Most of the time he let others talk, nodded absently, and concentrated on his glass. Only now and then would he throw in a word that hit the mark.

He did not even glance at the Anschluss ballot. He just growled and said, "Farce," without surprise.

Should one go, I wondered, to cast a "no" vote? The idea seemed to amuse Roth. "Go and try," he suggested, sounding much like the S.S. man at the Vienna Westbahnhof. What he was putting on paper now was not the usual fine script; I saw him draw crosses, rather—scores, hundreds of tiny crosses aligned in neat rows as in a military cemetery. Then, with small strokes, he broke them up into swastikas.

"By now the outcome is presumably in print," he said, crumpling the paper. He dropped it into the metal ashtray, lit a cigarette, and used the same match to set fire to the

34

paper ball. A mound of ashes was all that remained of the
cemetery.

By now the result was presumably in print . . . ahead of
time. I thought that over, walking through the silent streets
of the *quartier* at dawn, and for the first time I was glad
to have left Vienna.

"Amid the rejoicing of the masses," said the reports, the
outcome of the plebiscite was announced at the Vienna
Konzerthaus on April 11: 99 per cent to 1 for the big
"Yes." The meaning, as officially explained to us, was that
Austria would "now belong to Germany and its Führer for
all eternity."

In France we heard the tiny 1 per cent praised as "the
first courageous act of an Austrian resistance movement."
We saw something else in it: a Nazi trick that fully served its
purpose—to lend credibility abroad to the 99 per cent. Not
many thought as clearly and consistently as Roth, who called
the "vote" a farce from the beginning.

For the Nazis also used the farce to put a properly tight
rein on their new subjects. The "homecomers into the Reich"
got their first lesson in discipline. William Shirer, the American newsman to whom Nazi sources had foretold the exact
vote figures, visited a polling place in Vienna Sunday afternoon
and saw, as he wrote later, that "wide slits in the corner of
the polling booths gave the Nazi election committee
sitting a few feet away a good view of how one voted. In
the country districts few bothered—or dared—to cast their
ballots in the secrecy of the booth; they voted openly for all
to see." In some places eight or ten "party comrades," flanked
by S.A. men with fixed bayonets, sat at the table where voters
were handed a pencil to mark the open ballot form.

"I know, because I lived through it," a woman voter of
that day wrote on its thirtieth anniversary. "Anyone failing
to show up was fetched to the polls by S.A. in specially
requisitioned private cars (my own car was used for the

purpose). It was impossible not to vote." And she closed: "If I am now charged with lack of courage, I can only say that we knew exactly what was happening even then in the concentration camps."

One also knew that thousands of Austrians had been arrested in the days before the vote. I got a carefully worded note from my stepmother: My father was visiting my brother; she herself had lost her passport. . . . She must have taken part in the plebiscite, I gathered. I knew how she felt; I could understand how she had had to vote.

We began hearing of suicides. Few Austrians were still coming out, but travel by citizens of the successor states to the old Danubian monarchy was not interfered with. Our publisher friend Paul von Zsolnay, with his Hungarian passport, brought the latest news from Vienna: His managing director, half-Jewish, and a half-Jewish secretary had killed themselves rather than vote; an author of the house, a former major in the Imperial Army, had also put a bullet through his brain. In retrospect I shuddered at my idea of going back to cast a "no" vote.

Egon Friedell, the witty culture historian and actor, had jumped out of a window in Vienna. It had not been because of the plebiscite, from which he, as a "full Jew," was excluded anyway. In fact, he seemed to have acted under a misapprehension. From his window he had seen S.S. men enter the house, but not, as it turned out, for him; they were after someone else a flight below. By the time the other person was taken away, Friedell's body lay on the sidewalk.

We ourselves seemed to have been given a period of grace, but it was no more. Austria was now the Ostmark of the Third Reich, and the German consulate in Paris was exchanging Austrian passports for new German ones, with or without a "J," for Jew, beneath the swastika. So far the necessity was not inexorable; thanks to Miklas's stubbornness, France had not yet recognized the Anschluss. We had

36

the option of having an "ex" inserted before "Austrian" on our passports by the prefecture and running around as "*ex-autrichiens*" until the passports ran out. Heaven knew what would become of us then. Former Austrian politicians in Paris were busily founding committees but could not get together on a government in exile.

Of Schuschnigg's cabinet, only Zernatto had fled, traveling under a false name, with false papers. He finally reached Paris, but we did not see him. We cheered a swiftly spreading rumor that he had brought out the Fatherland Front treasury—"a charge contrasting so grotesquely with my situation," he wrote, "that for all my bitterness I sometimes burst out laughing."

Zernatto wrote and wrote. He wrote *The Truth about Austria*. The introduction sounded almost apologetic: "In this book I have tried to present the Austrian events objectively. I know I have not always succeeded. . . . One must remember that I had to write it homeless and penniless, without essential materials, in hurried flight. One must remember that my friends and comrades were slandered, plundered, persecuted, and incarcerated by the Nazis."

He dedicated his book "to all those who believe in Austria." The book was ours. Like the works of Horvath and Roth, it was printed in Holland—"Copyright 1938 by Guido Zernatto, Paris." It was written "from a heart filled with indomitable love for my country, from which I have been driven, but which I'll never stop loving, loving, loving."

Five years later—two years before the end of World War II would have enabled him to return home—the poet and ex-secretary of state Guido Zernatto died in New York of a "broken heart," according to his doctors. He was thirty-nine years old.

The Fatherland Front treasury had been seized by the Nazis. It was a pity; in Paris the money could have served better ends. Had Zernatto brought it along, there would have been no need for the collection the Austrian relief committee was just taking up, for example.

The police had sought the committee's help in identifying a mysterious stranger who was under arrest. The dilapidated young man spoke an oddly guttural language that no Frenchman understood, and he possessed a rifle, so the police picked him up. He also failed to carry papers of any kind. Our Austrians quickly discovered the truth: The bearded youth spoke Tyrolean dialect. When the Germans marched into the Tyrol, right by his house, he had remembered Schuschnigg's patriotic broadcast, gotten his rifle, and fired out the window; he hadn't hit anyone, though. Still, the only thing had been for him to disappear as fast as possible over the mountains.

After adventurous detours, not unlike Zernatto's, this solitary specimen of armed resistance had ended up in the hands of the Parisian *flics*, who did not know what to do with him. To the committee he even identified himself, after a fashion: Our Tryolean was a tailor. Now contributions were sought to help the valiant tailor, and the drive was so successful that he was soon able to set up shop in a little room on Montparnasse and start mending our clothes, for few of us could afford new ones.

"Everyone needs clothes," said Walter Mehring accusingly. "Compared with books——"

"I–" said Joseph Roth, sneering, "I compare my hotel bills with my publisher's statements. Book-publishing is an odd business. You live on losses. That must be very hard, considering that I can't even live on my advances."

Everyone of us wondered at times how he or she was living at all. Some earlier refugees had still been able to bring money along and had started businesses of their own. Some were helped by refugee committees, and others, like most of our friends, were able to work as free-lance writers. Carli and I tried desperately to go on with our literary agency, but there was hardly any free market left for us. Yet we remained quite cheerful. One day a new, very pretty blonde came up to Mehring in a café: "How wonderful to meet you!" she said, blushing.

She was an actress who lived in a little hotel nearby, and she loved Mehring's poems. She knew them all by heart and would recite them at every possible and impossible opportunity, she said and began: " 'Cling to your sweetheart when you're cold and daunted; let her warm breath thaw out your frozen cells—and by imps of curiosity be haunted, whose nightly carousing fills the dormer housing of the little hotels. . . .' " Everyone laughed. She was certainly one of us.

Next day, on the Rue Monsieur le Prince, Walter and I ran into an old acquaintance, a Viennese movie director. "Mehring, you haunt me!" he called from half a block away, came close, and continued in a confidential whisper. "Look, I'm in bed with a delightful young woman—and what does she do? She recites me your 'Little Hotels'!"

"Oh," said Mehring, looked into the air, snapped his fingers as if to take a picture—and named the girl, enjoying the other's bafflement.

It did no harm that the secret was out. The actress and the director stayed together, though not for some time as man and wife. They made up for it later in Hollywood, but the French would grant no marriage licenses to people with our ever-expiring papers.

Marrying was one of many things beyond our grasp.

CHAPTER 3

Champs-Élysées

"You've got to stay at least five days—" I hastily added the postscript to my reply to Horvath's letter from Amsterdam. He had asked me to reserve a room in our hotel; in a few days he would be in Paris. We'll see Odon again. . . . I could hardly wait, could not think beyond that moment.

He arrived on May 28 in the best of spirits. "I'm just passing through," he announced as soon as he was off the train. Paris would be a stopover on his way to America—some uncle there had sent him an affidavit, and in Hollywood a number of friends were waiting, among them the charming wife of a producer, a Marlene Dietrich type. Odon had seen her to the boat in Holland.

In Paris he was planning to meet Armand Pierhal, his French translator, who had already started work on *The Age of the Fish*, which Plon would publish; a possible

41

French-American coproduction of a film based on that novel had to be discussed with the director Robert Siodmak; negotiations with other French publishers were also pending; and there was an agent, a Russian woman, whom Odon wanted to see again.

"All in five days?" I asked, delighted. "That won't be enough."

We went to the Armenian bistro next to our hotel. Watching Odon happily munch the strongest paprikas again and wash them down with red wine made me feel transported back to Vienna's Griechenbeisl. He had traveled far since March, since our separation in Vienna. First to Czechoslovakia to visit Lydia St. Clair, an actress who worshipped him even when her own name shone in lights on Broadway, and to meet his fiancée, a pretty blonde named Vera; then to Zurich, to see other friends; and finally, via Brussels, to his publisher in Amsterdam. But over wine and paprikas it seemed as if we had been together only yesterday and nothing had changed.

"*Prost.*" Odon raised his glass and drank to Paris. This month's end would give his life its most decisive turn; a gypsy in Amsterdam had read that in his palm. We clinked glasses. There were two sides to such a turn, of course; the next few days, he said pensively, would call for caution. "Why are people afraid in dark woods? Why not in the street?" And he cast a wary eye on the blinking lights in the dark Rue Monsieur le Prince.

Odon was very superstitious. He hesitated to go out alone after that. He regarded May 31 as the crucial date, and on that day—it was a Tuesday—Carli had to accompany him everywhere: to Montmartre, for instance, to meet Ernst Aufricht, who had put on the original production of Brecht's *Three-Penny Opera* in Berlin and was now full of hopes for Horvath's plays in Paris.

"This is my lucky town," Odon told us at the bistro the evening of the thirty-first. Visibly relieved to have come unscathed through the critical period, he had decided to extend his visit. We drank *vin rosé* and made plans. Tomorrow he was going to meet Siodmak for lunch on the Champs-Élysées—would I like to come along? Pierhal was expecting him the day after tomorrow; the translation was making progress, and the agent, entranced with Odon, saw further chances for the novels. The really decisive turn might come from Aufricht; he expected the plays, which had been shelved since Hitler's advent, to be worldwide hits, like the novels. The more *rosé* we drank, the rosier our views of the situation.

Odon talked more, and more animatedly, than was his habit. He began to talk of his new novel, called *Adieu Europe*. Quite personally, as a writer about to emigrate to America, he had started it—on the blank paper that was "so terribly white." But this time he would go beyond the first person of his first few books, would go into other characters and speak out of the mouths of many, as in a play.

At the time this seemed like a new idea; decades had to pass before this form became fashionable in modern fiction. And only after the downfall of the Third Reich would Odon's plays be revived by a new generation to project the image of his days—a prophetic, translucent, enduringly valid image—in the form of today, in a way leading up to plays like those of Harold Pinter. World history confirmed his *Tales from the Vienna Woods*, and it survived the confirmation; it is back home in the Vienna Woods, rooted in the soil of Viennese farce and fancy, soaring above reality to the theatrical empyrean where the stars "will still hang high when we're laid low," as Odon put it in his play.

The last night of May, 1938, we spent drinking together until dawn, first at the bistro, then in the hotel with Carli. We took a couple of bottles to Odon's room and sat smoking and drinking and smoking. Odon scribbled doggerel on an empty cigarette box:

43

What's counterfeit will perish,
Its reign now is a hoax—
What's genuine we cherish,
Although today it croaks.

"There'll be a day of reckoning for millions of Germans,"
he said thoughtfully. "Some forty millions. . . ."

Carli jumped up. "Not even twenty millions are real Nazis!
Not even ten millions!"

The game went on until Carli beat a worried retreat. "Say,
five millions," Odon called after him, splitting the last difference. With his big, slightly bulging eyes he scrutinized himself in the wall mirror. "What do women see in me?" he
asked. "Am I so demonic?" It seemed to discomfit him.

I shrugged helplessly, looking at the tall, broad figure. It
was always the same. There was about him a kind of invisible
wall that you tried vainly to penetrate. His own inner world
cut him off from the outside world; he was under some
inner compulsion that seemed to govern him as well as his
characters.

To meet him was to like him. Most women were spell-
bound by him; but they came and went, and he remained
alone. "Tangential experiences," said Csokor, the friend who
seemed to get closest to him. "You touch at one point and
lose each other in infinity. . . ."

"Love is just a fixed idea," Odon had explained to me once;
it was now two years since I had inscribed the line for him in
a gift copy of my first novel. They would find the book
among his things in Paris.

"You still love me?" he asked abruptly and sat down facing me across the table with the bottle of wine. I did not
quite know what to say. Once before, at the Café Museum
in Vienna, he had faced me across such a table, and I had not
found an answer then either. How long ago? I could not tell
exactly. It was so long ago, I thought, it can't be true any
longer.

"Don't be shocked," Odon said that time at the Café Museum. "I'm getting married next week." It was the morning after an all-night session, and on the table between us lay a blue necktie I had brought him, with a card: "Blue morning wish. . . ."

The necktie too would show up in his hotel drawer, unlikely as it might seem on that last night of May. Playing about our glasses were "imps of memory"; the last bottle was still half full of wine when I got up. "Stay awhile," said Odon.

I hesitated. I was afraid that everything might start all over.

"Wouldn't a Hungarian passport be good for you?" he asked gaily. "After all, you have no nationality now."

The allusion made me laugh. For the passport had been the cause of his sudden proposal to Maria Elsner, a musical-comedy star about to be barred from the German stage as a Jew. Her brother told Horvath about it and added that the ban did not apply to foreigners—whereupon Odon, in a letter to Berlin, offered Maria his hand and nationality. I heard all this only later, after the month-old marriage had been dissolved by mutual consent.

Ringing after me from the Café Museum was only one sentence, clearly audible if not quite intelligible: "Between us, of course, there'll be no change. . . ." How could that be so after his marriage? This seemed impossible to me. Furious honking tore me out of my thoughts—I had almost been run over. Eventually I got home to my garret, which I was then sharing with a friend named Margot. Odon liked her too; we were a frequent trio. I had not said a word about the Café Museum when she left on a date that night.

Alone, I carefully closed all the windows, opened the gas jets, and lay on the couch. It was a pleasant feeling. The thought of the grotto ride in the Vienna Prater made me smile; Odon had often taken me to the amusement park, and on the grotto ride he would laugh when I screamed at the touches of ice-cold, wet, dead fingers. There was no reason to scream now, not even to please Odon—and I thought of the play we had meant to write together, based upon my story "*L'Inconnue de la Seine.*" We both found the smile of the famous death mask intriguing. Nothing came of the collaboration, though, for Odon's *Inconnue* soon had a life of her own and went her own way, like all his characters. It would have pleased me to show her smile now, but nothing came of that either.

It was impossible to resent anything Odon did. I never saw him other than friendly, helpful, cheerful. "That's the girl who wanted to kill herself because of me," he said on occasion, as if it were inconceivable. And we made fun of it. I resented only Margot's telling him about her early return that night, when she had found me lying on the couch in the gas-filled room and had rushed to open all the windows.

In retrospect it did seem funny, this concatenation of the accidents that fate is made of. And when dawn broke over the roofs of Paris as it had over Vienna, once upon a time, I found the answer to his question. It was his own line: "Love is just a fixed idea."

We finished the bottle and cheerfully said good night, leaving two half-filled glasses on the table.

I took a long time falling asleep. No sooner had I left Odon than I yearned to be with him. My eyes were shut, but I plainly saw his face.

"I didn't know you were staying here too," I whispered in his ear. We were not in the little Parisian hotel but in one in Munich. Odon was laughing again. Wasn't it hilarious that we had spent a week in the same house—on the same floor, in fact—without knowing it?

If only they could be held onto, these accidents of fate. . . . There were pictures dancing behind my closed lids: the carnival of 1933 in Munich, when a Chinese masker swept me into a *chambre séparée* and turned out to be my friend

Margot, while Thomas Mann's daughter Erika and another actress vanished with Horvath until we all met at the same *weisswurstkeller* at 6 A.M.; and the cabaret that people jammed each night to laugh at Hitler in *The Ass Is Loose*— only two weeks before he seized power, but we didn't know that and enjoyed the skit hugely, Odon and I. "You're sure you'll come?" I asked, snuggling close. We had the keys to the ski hut of Walter Tschuppik, a newspaper friend of his, and Margot and I were to go up ahead and wait at the hut for him and Tschuppik.

Neither came, though. We returned to Munich and were greeted by swastika flags. Editor Tschuppik, of the *Muenchner Neueste Nachrichten*, was in "protective custody," we heard; Horvath had fled. What we saw was the S.A. marching a prominent Jewish lawyer in his underwear down the main business street of Munich.

Later a postcard from Odon called me to Salzburg, but I did not find him there. A writer friend knew he had gone to the station to meet me and had not been seen since. Odon, Odon. . . .

In Vienna I found him again. He did not know what had gotten into his mind in Salzburg, or where he had been—most likely on some train. It had been on a train too that he once read a news item about a murder, thought he had committed it, and promptly got off to surrender to the police. They laughed at him, for he had never been near the place of the crime.

We laughed too, Odon and I. The big, bulging eyes were fixed on me: "Am I so demonic?" I tried to grab him in the dark, to hold him—then I lost my balance and fell, plunged into the void in which he seemed to have vanished. I tried to scream but could not manage a sound—and when I struck bottom, I was in my bed in the Hôtel de l'Univers in Paris. It was noon. I had overslept.

Mme. Boucher had a note for me: Odon had left for his

lunch date with Siodmak; I could join them at the Cinéma Champs-Élysées for the matinee of Walt Disney's *Snow White*. Otherwise dinner at the bistro, as usual. *Au revoir.*

In the lobby I met Mehring. He had had breakfast with Odon at the Café Mathieu on the boulevard. "It was strange," Walter said, musing. "What is an anti-Semite in the first place?" Odon had asked him. "Does he enjoy it, or is he just scared?" And at that moment, out of the blue, a lightning bolt had struck the nearby Panthéon.

I had slept through this too. The heat was oppressive that Wednesday; at the subway entrance, "DIRECTION CHAMPS-ÉLYSÉES," a searing wave of air drove me back. "You can have a stroke down there," I said to Mehring.

In the evening a cool breeze stirred the trees of the Luxembourg. Carli and I waited at the bistro as usual. It got pretty late. Was Odon merely unpunctual, or had he forgotten?

Carli went to the hotel to ask if there had been a call for us from M. Horvath. He came back chalk-white. "Police called —for you," he stammered. "Come, we must get to Odon. . . ." He drew me into the street.

"Where is he?"

"At the hospital. An accident," Carli replied.

"The accident," said my lips, and in passing I picked up Odon's mail for him. When I came out of the hotel with it, Carli had called a taxi, a rare extravagance for us. "Is there such a hurry?" I asked, getting in. Carli shrugged.

The sun was sinking like a fireball behind the Arch of Triumph. Tears gleamed in Carli's eyes. "Is he dead?" I stammered. Carli did not answer. The taxi stopped at the hospital.

Men in white met us. We asked for Horvath. "Are you relatives?"

"Friends," said Carli.

"Monsieur Horvath is dead," it came back. Carli held my arm.

In a white room Odon lay under a white sheet and did not move. "He's alive," I cried, "he's alive!" But he did not move.

"Killed instantly," I heard and saw the bloodstains under his head.

"Murderers," I screamed at the white coat. Carli held me back.

"A falling tree killed him," said the white one, probably a doctor. A sudden gust had snapped one of the chestnut trees at the Rond-Point like a twig. Everyone else had escaped; only this passerby had caught a branch in the neck, having run in the direction of the fall, apparently. The ambulance had found him face down under the tree and rushed him to the hospital. Dead on arrival.

I had to identify him. He had carried no papers at all except my letter with his name and my address—hence the police call for me. The open letter was returned to me. A bloodstain ran through the postscript: "You've got to stay at least five days—"

It was the fifth day.

The night passed somehow. First we called Robert Siodmak; he almost fainted by the phone, having left Odon outside the theater in the best of spirits. In Zurich we reached Odon's brother, Lajos. "No, no," he cried into the phone, "not a tree—it must have been Nazis!" He managed to say that he would inform their parents and also Vera, Odon's fiancée—I should reserve rooms for them all at our hotel.

The proprietress wept. She was going to pray for Odon. In the lobby we met Mehring, who broke down at the news, sobbing uncontrollably. Then he undertook to speak to the police and to some reporters who had already come sniffing round. Horvath's room had to be padlocked; nothing must be touched until the family came.

The half-filled wine glasses were still on the table, and on the corner desk lay the first page of the unfinished *Adieu Europe*:

> Many plans go through my head, and the blank paper is so terribly white. But in this solitude here I am sure things will crystallize.
>
> I love the sea.
>
> It comes with new waves, over and over again —and I do not know yet whether it will be a comedy or a tragedy.
>
> Yesterday's storm was more violent. The nets tore overnight, and one boat did not return. Maybe it will emerge in a year's time, with black sails, and ride the waters as a specter without a soul.
>
> I do not know yet.

The morning edition of the Paris *Figaro* carried this item:

> A storm which broke over Paris yesterday caused several accidents. In the Champs-Élysées it toppled a chestnut tree. Seven persons managed to get to safety, except for one Hungarian, who was killed.
>
> In the Channel the same storm overturned a fishing boat. The entire crew drowned. The unmanned boat foundered on our shore this morning.

Without a soul. . . . The room was locked, and at the Gare du Nord I stood awaiting Horvath's parents and his brother. I recognized Lajos at once; he looked like a smaller Odon. The parents followed, the old baron supporting himself with a cane. The mother, a handkerchief pressed to her eyes, was weeping in silence.

They wanted to go straight to Odon. He lay as the day before; only his cheeks seemed somewhat hollower, which made him smile. The mother seemed to calm down at his peaceful expression. The father never left her side. The brother was asked to sign for the overcoat Odon had worn, a light raincoat with bloodstains across the back.

A small package fell out when the coat was handed over. Lajos picked it up and hastily pocketed it. The contents turned out to be photos of the kind you can buy at every stand along the Left Bank: naked girls in diverse poses of love, with men and with each other. "I don't want Mother to see," Lajos whispered to me as he hid the pictures. Was it a comedy or a tragedy?

A man with a wooden leg came to our hotel, where the family had settled. He was dressed in black, wore a bowler hat, and introduced himself as an undertaker; he had read in the papers about the horrible accident and wished to offer his services. His price, which I translated to the parents, seemed fair; they gave him the down payment he requested, and the baroness ordered a special flower arrangement and said she would get a priest.

The man in black seemed moved. He had lost his leg but found his intended in Germany after World War I, he said, with a side glance at me. After another expression of his sympathy for us, including me as the "intended," he withdrew with a bow and a promise to do his best.

Not wishing to disappoint the good man, I did not explain that the girl Odon had called his fiancée was still on a train to Paris. I was going to meet her train too; Vera Liessem and I were good friends despite the rather strange beginning of our friendship. "I've brought a fiancée along"—this was the first I heard of her existence, again at some Vienna coffeehouse, the first time I saw Odon after his divorce. He had just returned from Berlin; in his mind a book was hatching, and he had wanted a first-hand look at the Nazis. They were "beastly," he told me, but I was going to like his fiancée.

A few days later, at a lecture of Franz Theodor Csokor's, I made Vera's acquaintance. Csoker called her the Cat. She was pretty, blond, born in Hamburg, and after the introductions she appraised me with an expert glance and turned to

Odon: "So she's what you make such a fuss about?" Odon guffawed; this was even more fun than the grotto ride. And I was pleased to hear that he had made a fuss about me.

The next morning I called Vera. "Let's not be played against each other," I proposed, and she agreed immediately. To follow Odon she had quit a cabaret job in Berlin, but she quickly found one in Vienna. Soon she was regularly appearing at Der Liebe Augustin and joining Odon, Csokor, and me at the Griechenbeisl after her performance.

Odon would read us passages from the new book. We heard him speak like a schoolteacher to children who had lost their way in a Nazi-ruled land. Suddenly things were not all "beastly" any more. Truth spoke out of conscience, even out of a priest who said God was "the most terrible thing in the world." For the first time we heard Odon speak of God— but the teacher in his book no sooner unmasked the lie than he was driven out of his homeland. At the end of the book he would go "to the blacks," away from the "youth without God."

This was the book's title in Germany, where it was banned at once, only to go round the world then as *Jeunesse sans Dieu* and *The Age of the Fish*. "In this work of yours you have seen God, after your fashion," Csokor wrote in a "last greeting" to Odon, "but to see God is to die." There was no chance for Csokor to come from Poland to Paris and accompany his friend on his last journey, but Vera came. We embraced wordlessly. She had been crying.

"Fatty," she kept repeating incredulously on the ride to the hotel. It had been her name for Odon. "Fatty. . . ." She had to laugh through her tears, which offended the mother, who could not understand the underlying compulsion—the same that ruled Odon's characters and had ruled him.

In the night after her arrival Vera knocked on my door. She was distraught. "I can't sleep," she whispered when I opened; "Fatty is always there."

I drew her into my room. "Stay here. I'd like to see him too." The bed was broad enough for the two of us. Vera was soon fast asleep; I stared into the night, waiting, but Odon did not come.

Early the next morning we rode to St. Ouen Cemetery in a long taxi procession. The whole Parisian refugee colony came to the funeral: Franz and Alma Werfel, from their hotel near the Opéra; Roth and his Round Table; Siodmak, the last of us to have seen Odon alive. Our peg-legged friend had brought the flower arrangement and a second undertaker to assist him. A Hungarian priest the baroness had found was carrying a handful of Hungarian earth to fling into Odon's grave.

"All that was home once and the bit of fatherland"—once again Mehring's "Emigrants' Song" fitted the occasion. The last stanza kept running through my mind: "That's what the emigrant lugs over hill and dale and bog and wave and, when his life's visa expires, to the grave." Our voluble poet sat very still in the cab now between Vera and me.

We passed a flea market with a little amusement park attached, with calliopes and tent shows as Odon had loved them in the Vienna Prater; the sounds pursued us all the way to the cemetery, into which the two undertakers led us by a back door—because at the main gate, they said, there was construction work going on. The grave was right there, separated only by the cemetery wall from railroad tracks that ran along the cemetery and into the world. The rumble and the whistles of passing trains could be heard all through the service. Odon had been so fond of trains.

It started raining. Slowly, gently, the drops fell from the dark sky into the open grave. My face was wet. The priest recited the Lord's Prayer like the confessor in the cathedral scene from *Tales from the Vienna Woods*. I had to think of

Odon's stage direction: "The bells fall silent, and the world is very still."

"Amen," the priest said. And somewhere in the stillness I heard the girl from Odon's cathedral: "If there is a God—what do you intend to do with me, God? . . . I am not a bad girl—do you hear me? What do you intend to do with me, God?"

The world was very still, empty, and dark. Then voices rang out in the darkness: "A strange death," Franz Werfel, pondering, said at the end of his eulogy. "Why did Odon von Horvath have to die? Had he the word on his lips, perhaps —had he in his mind the sentence that must not be spoken and written down until time is fulfilled?"

"A tree killed him," declared Walter Mehring, pale, sharp-tongued, staccato-voiced. " 'There grows a tree, a tall tree on the edge of a high plain,' it says in his novel *Child of Our Time*. The tree killed him. . . ."

The drops kept falling. No lightning struck, no leaf stirred; only the trains rumbled on and on. We stood in the rain until the grave was closed and the white flowers lay on the fresh earth. Then we survivors left as we had come in, sneaking out the back door of the cemetery, and the taxis took us past the flea market and back into the city.

The following morning we had another visit from the police. This time they wanted to know about our undertaker. He was in jail. Out of special consideration for us the arrest had been deferred until after the funeral.

The man with the peg leg, we heard, was a swindler. Whenever the press reported a fatal accident, especially one involving a foreigner, he would approach the bereaved family, get a down payment, and disappear. He had been playing this game for years and had been caught now only because for once he had actually arranged the funeral. "An old crook," said the detectives.

I explained the matter to the parents. The baron was indignant: Should the man's one good deed be so ill rewarded? The baroness insisted on giving him the very best reference possible; it might mitigate the sentence, the *flics* assured her, taking careful notes. Brother Lajos, not satisfied with that, got the address of the jail and sent money and goodies to the kindhearted confidence man.

The gifts were returned as undeliverable. We never heard of our peg-legged friend again. To me he would always be a Horvath figure, a character from a Horvath play, come to life to bury his creator.

We scanned Odon's manuscripts to prepare a reading, a Horvath memorial to be held while his parents were with us. This left little time and posed considerable difficulties, since the German-speaking emigrés were split into all conceivable groups—from Left to Right, from Communists to monarchists. Horvath had belonged to no group; like his characters he remained an individual. "I have no goal but one: the unmasking of consciousness," he wrote. And over the *Tales from the Vienna Woods* he put a motto: "Nothing gives as great a sense of infinity as stupidity."

The stupidities had to be kept from the parents; they were to be spared all excitement. Every time we got someone to accept, someone else would back out. "If you do not exclude the Communists," Mehring declared, full of righteous wrath, "I'm out."

I discussed the problem with Carli in the subway, in German. "If he spoils it," I said, bristling and incautiously raising my voice, "I'm going to kill Mehring!" A diminutive gentleman in our car looked daggers at me and got off at the next stop. Carli put his finger on his lips.

At the Hôtel de l'Univers the phone rang for Mehring. His journalist friend Friedrich Sternthal was on the line, whispering, "Mehring, a red-haired wench and a black-haired delinquent plan to assassinate you."

"That's all right; I know them" was Walter's cheerful response. And before nightfall he brought us together with Sternthal, a living literary encyclopedia who would end up as a *Britannica* editor in Chicago. He was as small and delicate as Mehring himself and equally addicted to berets. One often saw them together in the crooked streets of the *quartier*, wandering from bar to bar in deep discussion.

The Horvath memorial was saved, in the end, by Joseph Roth. He had not spoken at the grave; standing outdoors in the rain for an hour was too difficult for a man in his state. He had come to the hotel to call on the parents, though. Lajos told us about it: Roth came in, every inch a retired Austro-Hungarian officer, kissed the baroness's hand, bowed to the baron, clicked his heels—and left without a word, swallowing tears. Now he consented to preside over the memorial and to bring the knights of his Round Table, along with his customary water glass. It looked as innocent beside him as the other glasses did beside the rest of the speakers, and as at the Tournon he took frequent sips whose nature was known to initiates only.

In the front row Horvath's father and mother sat listening, equally moved by speeches of Austrian Rightists, German Leftists, and French Catholics like Jacques Maritain and Pierhal, whom the parents felt they understood despite the unfamiliar language. Pierhal had not seen Odon anymore, had only heard his voice over the telephone, said the translator; but now he was talking with him every day in *Jeunesse sans Dieu*.

It was the family's express wish that Vera and I both take part in the memorial. I read the one finished page of *Adieu Europe* and the letter from Warsaw in which Csokor bade Odon farewell: "You and your work will be summoned as key witnesses on behalf of things of this world. But the great, solemn manner of your death makes you a key witness for something higher, for eternal truth against ephemeral reality, for eternal justice against human judgments."

I stepped down. Vera replaced me on the platform. "Two fiancées, as at the funeral," murmured Roth, stifling a chuckle.

Vera did not hear him—her eyes were on Odon's book, from which she was going to read—but I struck back. "At your funeral, Herr Roth, we'll be missing," I told him.

Vera read from the last chapter of *Child of Our Time*. "The snowman," she said, and went on:

> "It is cold." That remains my first memory.
> The night goes by; slowly another day comes.
> I am full of snow and do not move.
> A young woman comes with a small child.
> The child sees me first, claps its hands, and cries,
> "Look, Mama! A snowman!"
> Mama looks at me and her eyes widen . . . and I
> hear her scream: "Help! Help!"

There were tears in Vera's eyes. I heard her read of how a policeman comes and takes a good look at the snowman and concludes, "Yes, he's sure frozen stiff. He's had it"—and how the child turns again and again to look curiously at the snowman.

Vera read and wept:

> Just keep looking!
> A snowman sits on the bench; he is a soldier.
> And you, you'll grow up and will not forget the
> soldier.
> Or will you?
> Don't forget him, don't forget him!
> For he gave his arm for a shit.
> And once you're full grown, there are going to be
> other days, perhaps, and your children will tell you:
> That soldier was quite simply a common killer—
> then don't you too call me names.

Mind this: He did not know how else to help
himself; he was a child of his time.

The thirtieth anniversary of Odon's death was observed
recently at another memorial, this one in Vienna, with Franz
Theodor Csokor presiding, as Roth had done in Paris. I was
summoned from New York to speak about Odon; Vera, now
a German radio-TV editor, was too busy to come, and in her
place Helmut Qualtinger read from *Child of Our Time*. He
is a young actor lately voted "the most interesting Austrian"
by the foreign correspondents in Vienna and written up in
The New York Times. He owed this praise to his creation of
a character named Herr Karl, an unforgettable specimen of
the banality and folksiness of evil—a full-length, full-face
portrait of what seemed like a dozen Horvath types rolled
into one.

Qualtinger had been in grade school at the time of Horvath's death. After the war he discovered Horvath's work and
remained under his spell. At the close of the Vienna memorial he spoke as Snowman: "And once you're full grown
. . . your children will tell you: That soldier was quite simply
a common killer. . . ."

Many young people were in the audience, many who had
not yet been born when the great slaughter occurred. They
had standing room only, and at the end they stood cheering
Qualtinger, who took a few quick bows and disappeared.
He had to rush to a nearby theater to put on his makeup for
Tales from the Vienna Woods, where they were driving
Odon's Viennese girl to despair again, night after night,
with Papa Qualtinger wallowing in self-pity: "Is there nothing I'll be spared?"

A motto framed the stage: "Nothing gives as great a sense
of infinity as stupidity." The theater had been sold out for
weeks. "How did you get seats when even I was unable to?"

Qualtinger asked Csokor and me when we joined him for a drink after the performance. That was another Horvath story.

The theater management had turned down Csokor's request; I tried the box office and every ticket agent in town and finally gave up hope. Exhausted, I came back to my little hotel near St. Stephen's, the one with the plaque that tells passersby that a poet lived there at the turn of the century. I rang the bell. The night clerk opened. "Would you like two seats for the Volkstheater tomorrow?" he asked, handing me my key.

I doubted my ears. "For *Tales from the Vienna Woods?*"
He nodded, reaching into a drawer.
"How much?" I asked uncertainly.
"Reduced," I heard. "Half price. Good seats, though."
He showed me the tickets. Orchestra, third row. . . .
"Where—how did you get them?" I stammered.
"Just happened," said the clerk. And that was that.
Qualtinger looked deeply into his glass. "I sure didn't send them. *Prost.* . . ."

The story made the rounds. I told it to Lajos von Horvath at a little café near his home. His hair was gray, but he still resembled his brother. "Of course, it was Odon who sent the tickets," he said.

He brought me a book one could not get anymore, a Horvath anthology edited by Csokor for an Austrian paperback series. The copy was inscribed to Lajos, and he made me promise to return it on my next Viennese trip. We said good-bye in front of the café, and I watched him head for home, step by laborious step, until I lost him round the corner.

His heart ailment had worsened lately. It was a memento of the great cold before Stalingrad; as a cog in Hitler's war machine, Lajos paid for the filial concern that had drawn him back to Germany some months after Odon's death. He never fully recovered from the Russian campaign. He was an artist, though, and he painted the unspeakable and brought the icy deaths of men and animals before the eyes of the living.

"The older generation will recall an exhibit at the Josefstadt Theater," the Vienna *Presse* wrote in summer, 1968, "and remember the impact of those canvases, the mastery with which Lajos von Horvath preserved the dread experiences from the retreat of his unit in winter, 1942." Yes, I remember. "None could fail to hear the indictment born of compassion with tormented creatures. In this basic attitude of mind and soul he was no mere blood kin of his brother, Odon."

He was. . . . Time comes to a stop. Puzzled, I read the enclosure—a death notice: "My dear husband, Herr Lajos von Horvath, Lieutenant of the Reserve, Signum Laudis in silver with swords, and holder of other medals and badges of honor, died on July 8, 1968, after a long illness."

In silver with swords. I had forgotten the medals. They may have been hidden somewhere beneath the canvases.

" 'It is cold,' " says the snowman. "That remains my first memory." And I see a dying in the snow. "He is a soldier. . . . Don't forget him, don't forget him!"

This soldier was our brother.

CHAPTER 4

Rest in View
of Ruin

"I feel as if Odon had died a second time," wrote Franz Theodor Csokor. And in Paris, in that summer of 1968, *Don Juan Comes Back from the War* was shown on television, the first Horvath play to be translated, and long articles in the papers told the story of how a tree had killed him in the City of Light on June 1, 1938.

The date was historic, but at first we did not notice. The shadow of Odon's death eclipsed all things. Only gradually, as if from far off, we began to hear the voices of the dark again.

On that June 1, British Prime Minister Neville Chamberlain announced that he would henceforth back Hitler's demand for the right of self-determination of the minorities in Czechoslovakia. As a result the Nazi barking on the air rose to a fortissimo that wakened even us. At the Café de Tournon we sat listening to a radio set wedged between bottles while

61

the *patronne* filled glasses and took them to Joseph Roth's table. Only Roth himself seemed unconcerned. He polished his phrases, punctuated them with sips from the water glass, and ignored the Nazi orators whose reverberations the radio hurled at our ears. "Like our folk comrades everywhere, we demand justice!" it quoted the boss of Czechoslovak Nazis, Konrad Henlein.

"Might as well come from Danzig." The comment, in Hermann Rauschning's strong Baltic accent, came from the corner where the former Nazi boss of Danzig was conferring with a fugitive from the Reich.

This man preferred to remain anonymous because in Germany he was under a death sentence. We called him K.G., the initials of one of his pseudonyms, and his connection with us was basically nonpolitical: He was infatuated with Vera Liessem. Like Lajos, Vera had remained in Paris after the Horvath parents left for home. Having shared a platform with men wanted by the Gestapo, she thought her name too might now be on its lists—and if so, a return to Prague, where she had last been working, was clearly not advisable. The flowers K.G. kept sending her brought no response from Vera. She just didn't like him.

K.G. also brought us a young Briton, a pale, angelic-looking pre-Raphaelite type who talked expertly of German troop deployments and Czech defense strategies and seemed altogether well informed. We called him Newday. He traveled a lot, without mentioning where he went—an Englishman, after all, could go where he pleased—and at times he foretold acts of sabotage, which never failed to happen.

Newday spoke German fluently, and so, it turned out now, did Manga Bell. Our lovely African queen had grown up in Hamburg, the daughter of a black trombonist and a girl from the waterfront; with the red rose in her hair she looked more like a Spanish woman. She would join the discussions in the corner, then disappear every so often, returning after an hour or two with lists that she gave to K.G.

One day he explained what it was all about: nothing more cryptic than addresses picked at random from German telephone directories. One used them for anti-Nazi propaganda mailings, K.G. said, and asked whether Mehring would like to write texts for the purpose. Walter modestly declined at once: "I'm just a poet."

K.G. turned to Carli and me: He urgently needed an assistant anyway for secretarial work. Carli accepted and began typing letters in his small room in Montparnasse. The money came as a godsend. Our sporadic sales of articles were too rare, and only now and then had we been able to sell translation rights of books, like those of my own Suttner biography to Holland and Scandinavia.

We never knew whether there would be a tomorrow. Many a time we were behind with our rent at the Hôtel de l'Univers, and often we had only a sandwich to eat instead of going to the cheap little Chinese restaurant around the corner, where you were lucky enough to get rice and tea at discretion.

As he now worked with K.G., Carli struck up a friendship with Newday of which the rest of us heard nothing but German student songs chanted to Newday's guitar behind locked doors. Such cheerful tunes as "Alt-Heidelberg" rang out there, under the roofs of Paris, and then at Heidelberg a munitions train might happen to blow up.

K.G. worried about Vera. He used to ask me if there was nothing she needed and how she could live without looking for a new job. I could put his mind at rest; according to a wish that Odon had expressed in an old letter, Lajos and Vera were sharing the income from his books. It was considerable, with *Youth without God* due to appear in France and sold, along with *Child of Our Time*, to England and even to America.

Roth kept working. When he looked up, his eyes passed over our heads and across the street to the old Hôtel Foyot, where he had lived for many years. It was being razed

now. Slowly but surely the old building turned into a
rubble pile. "Rest in View of Ruin," Roth wrote over an
article for a small emigré weekly published by the former
editor of one of Berlin's great magazines of letters and
opinion.

Roth wrote and drank, drank and wrote. "Unless you
stop drinking," his doctor warned him at the café, "your
days are numbered."

The writer stroked his damp moustache. "If I don't drink,
I can't write."

He did not rest in view of ruin. Carefully he covered
page after page with his pedantic handwriting. He had to
finish a novelette for his publisher in Amsterdam, the one
who had published Horvath's books; Lajos von Horvath was
to design the jacket for Roth's *Legend of the Holy Drinker*.
He showed us his sketch of little St. Thérèse of Lisieux, the
drinker's guardian and companion who takes him to her,
smiling, in the end. "May God give all us drinkers so easy
and sweet a death," Roth ended his legend.

"You must meet these new young people," said a journalist we knew. Georg Stoessler had just arrived from Vienna,
holding a Czech passport that had enabled him to get out;
now he was taking Carli and me across the boulevard to the
Hôtel Select, at 1 Place de la Sorbonne. From outside it
looked like any other hotel in the Latin Quarter. Inside we
found a new world.

Voices from the room Stoessler was heading for rang out,
lively and unintelligible, halfway down the stairs. A tall
blond Viking opened the door, patted Stoessler's back, and
shook our hands. Noticing that we knew hardly a word of
English, he switched to broken French to introduce us to his
pretty wife, who wore her dark hair parted in the middle,
madonna style, and to the rest of the multilingual company.

As around Roth at the Tournon, a motley crowd gathered here almost nightly around Lois and Eric Sevareid. If

at the café the link was fear of Hitler, at the Sevareids' it was to be young. Later we met other refugees at their place, but on that first evening only North and South Americans in their twenties sat at the table where Lois ladled out spaghetti from a huge bowl and poured cheap *vin ordinaire*. Eric came from Minnesota and was working as a reporter for the Paris *Herald*, the house organ of the American colony. Lois spent her days with a committee aiding sick and wounded American volunteers who had been fighting in the war in Spain. This was how Stoessler had come to know them. He too had volunteered to fight for the beleaguered Spanish republic, where Czechs too would be accepted; and while awaiting transportation to the battlefield, he hoped the Sevareids would put him up at the apartment they planned to rent the day they could afford it.

The interrupted discussion continued. It dealt with Spain, with the background of Francisco Franco's rebellion; unable to follow, I asked Stoessler to interpret. Eric did it himself. "Fascism means war," he repeated in French. "Sooner or later we'll all have to face it somewhere." And suddenly we were all talking a blue streak, understanding each other without knowing one another's language, because our thoughts were alike.

Spain was our business, we had heard Ernst Toller preach at the Tournon. The poet-playwright of the 1918 German revolution had been safely overseas in America—yet here he was, shuttling in and out of besieged Madrid, pleading the Loyalist cause, and raising money, millions, for the children orphaned on both sides. In New York, we heard, he was translated, published, lionized as the beau ideal of a literary radicalism that was coming into fashion over there; but the Spanish conflict had brought him back to Europe. And the American committee for which Lois Sevareid worked had been started by Ernest Hemingway, another magic name for those of us who had grown up with *A Farewell to Arms* and learned modern prose from *The Sun Also Rises*. The fiesta

had now turned into a bloody civil war, its setting into a
rifle range for Benito Mussolini and Adolf Hitler. By now,
though Hemingway's requiem to the tragedy was still unwritten, we knew "for whom the bell tolls."

Sevareid later wrote about our encounter. "Through many
nights, ever innumerable bottles of cognac, one listened to
the stories of what was happening in the central fortress of
the Fascists. You could not disbelieve—and you could not
quite believe. No effort of will or imagination could bring me
all the way into the world of the human spirit which they
had known," he wrote of us.

If this was so, we did not realize it. The young Americans
seemed to grasp all that we told them. We not only made
friends with them but also felt akin. And in no matter how
many languages the sign of fascism loomed menacingly on
the wall, we too were many—and so young that someday
the world must be ours.

"This was the basic motivating force for my generation,
perhaps for all my century," Eric wrote. He was all the way
in our world in those days, for all the newsman's skepticism
he professed in retrospect in his memoirs, titled after an
American poet's contention that brotherhood was "not so
wild a dream."

In vain the Sevareids and their friends racked their brains
about getting us to America. One night a colleague of Eric's,
Ted Meltzer, looked at his whiskey and then at me: "I could
marry you, Hertha," he drawled, "but my girl friend in St.
Paul would mind."

Ted was a giant, much taller even than Sevareid. When he
picked me up at my hotel, he had to stoop to pass through
the door. A Minnesotan like Eric, but of German descent, he
spoke bits of German, loathed the puritanism of his compatriots, and adored Paris—because it was not so puritanical,
I suppose.

He chose his own way to show me Paris. Of all its sights
the main attraction for him was the zoo of Vincennes—

specifically, the sea elephant in the big pool. Like an immense rock the colossus lay in the water, and when he huffed, it spilled over. Ted called him a philosopher.

Our visits to Vincennes were always timed so we could watch the feeding of the giant. The keeper came with a large bucket of fish and stepped on the back of the elephant, the elephant twisted his head all the way back, with an almost loving expression, and then the bucket was simply emptied into the wide-open maw. Ted looked on, full of envy. "I wish the good things in life would come to me like that," he used to say.

His whiskey did not, unfortunately. The Sevareids served only wine then, too weak a beverage for Ted; he generally took me to the Café Capoulade, on the Boulevard Saint-Michel, for drinks and to tell me about Charlotte, the girl friend in St. Paul. She had a good job in a department store, and one day—I had primped especially for him—he broke off in midsentence to examine me with a frown. "In America you'll have to dress better," he said.

"Don't worry; they won't let my kind travel anyway," I shot back furiously. "Cheers."

"Hertha," he said, "you're driving me out of my mind. The other night I dreamt I'd lost my U.S. passport."

I had to laugh. "And I dreamt I'd got one. . . ." Ours were the wild dreams.

One day we went to the Tournon and found Roth's chair empty. He was in the hospital. "A little attack; nothing serious," we were assured by his friend Morgenstern. Manga Bell said nothing. The *patronne*, who always cared so tenderly for Roth, poured drinks with a glum face. She had locked up his manuscripts in any event, on the correct assumption that no other objects in reach were as likely to cover his debts.

The radio brought sounds of Nuremberg, where the annual Nazi-party convention was drawing to a close. Bedlam seemed to reign behind the liquor bottles: jubilantly roaring masses, *Sieg Heil* choruses, the Führer's phrases abruptly ejaculated in between. "We—want—justice for the Sudeten Germans! Germans belong—to Germans! *Sieg—Heil!*"

Prague broadcast news of riots in the Sudetenland and of Czech governmental determination. Martial law had been proclaimed; Henlein had fled to the Reich. But at a flick of the dial you learned from the German radio broadcast that the Sudeten leader had been summoned by the Führer, who wished a firsthand report while pondering his historic decision. "Chewing rugs again," said Konrad Heiden, Hitler's biographer, who usually sat quietly in our midst and was reputed to know more about Hitler than the Führer himself knew.

Another turn of the dial gave you Radio Paris, loud and clear and tranquilizing. Premier Édouard Daladier's cabinet had discussed the Czech question and found no direct threat to peace. The tension would abate, and the commentator stressed that this view was shared by France's allies, with whom the government was in close touch, of course. Newday grinned; he knew that the British ambassador had been called out of the Opéra Comique last night to confer with Daladier.

"They'd better confer with Litvinov," said a lean, handsome man with dark horn-rimmed glasses. Erich Wollenberg had been a general of the Red Army and was now combining a fierce anti-Stalinism with the belief that everything depended on the Soviet Union, at least as long as the pro-Western Maxim Litvinov was its foreign minister.

What mattered more, East or West? The quarrel raged across the empty chair, for Roth alone knew how to reduce these antitheses to a common denominator. At his table Right and Left, monarchists, clerics, revolutionaries, used to join hands against Hitler; and when they finally laid Roth to rest the next spring, a priest without surplice read a Latin prayer while Jews said Kaddish and a black-and-yellow-ribboned wreath from His Apostolic Majesty, Otto von Hapsburg, lay beside a red-ribboned one inscribed, "To Comrade Roth."

In autumn, 1938, we sat without him for a few days only, and I wondered what he would have said when K.G. took violent issue with Wollenberg, when Rauschning rapped for order as though still presiding over the Danzig Senate. "The German High Command won't go along," the ex-Nazi announced authoritatively.

A moment's silence, a flicker of hope—we did not want war. We kept hoping for an inner upheaval, for "the other Germany" to turn the tables. Would the High Command do it?

"German generals do not make revolutions," scoffed our ex–Red general. The unwritten law he seemed to know by heart was promptly, sharply challenged, and a new dispute erupted, with words falling like blows. I ducked and looked out the window to see how much of the old hotel across the street had disappeared in the past twenty-four hours. A shadow moved across the wreckage—inaudibly, for at our table you could not hear your own voice, much less a taxi pulling up at the café.

Escorted by his two familiars, his old schoolmate and the dark woman he loved, Joseph Roth appeared on the threshold. Silence fell. Without a word, greeting us only with his glassy eyes, Roth headed for the vacant chair, sat down, nodded, and waved to the proprietress, who came hurrying up with the usual order.

The hand that reached for the water glass looked like a skeleton's. After the first sip Roth revived. The beaming *patronne* put his sequestered manuscripts before him on the table, and he drew his fountain pen and commenced writing.

"I tell you," he wrote, "one loses home after home. Here I sit, wandering, footsore, heart-weary, dry-eyed. Misery huddles beside me and keeps getting gentler and bigger. Pain stands still, grows vast and kindly; terror roars and can no longer terrify. And that precisely is the dismal part."

One night Roth returned to the table from one of his secretive phone calls looking more acidulous than ever. There was an interesting social note on Mr. Chamberlain, he said. The helmsman of the globe-girdling British Empire had wired Hitler a request for an audience.

Roth must be delirious, I thought, glancing at his glass; he doesn't know what he's saying. . . . As it turned out after the holocaust, Hitler was as stunned as we were. According to eyewitnesses, he found it hard to believe the humble wire. No one could doubt the facts of September 15, however, when a swarm of reporters and photographers saw Chamberlain land in Munich and board a train for Berchtesgaden. "It's just like Schuschnigg," it struck me when we learned of the pilgrimage.

A second Berchtesgaden burst upon us. At Hitler's mountain retreat the Briton was led to the very room where our Austrian chancellor had sat seven months earlier. Whether he too was forbidden to smoke remained unclear, but everybody quoted his impression of the Führer: "a man whose word can be relied upon."

And indeed, Hitler kept the sole promise he made at Berchtesgaden: to await another meeting before taking military steps. On the twenty-second of September he received Chamberlain again, this time at Godesberg, on the Rhine, and opened the talks with the announcement that German troops would enter the Sudetenland between the twenty-sixth and the twenty-eighth. "Is that an ultimatum?" Chamberlain stammered.

"By no means," the Führer replied. He was willing to extend the deadline—to October 1. "You are one of the few for whom I have ever done anything like this," he gravely assured Neville Chamberlain, and not till after the war did it become known from Wehrmacht files that the invasion had always been planned for the first of October.

On September 23 mobilization posters went up on Parisian walls and advertising pillars. The official statement cited France's obligation to her Czech ally, but in the semiofficial *Temps* we read at the same time that this was no legal commitment.

On the twenty-sixth Britain vowed to stand by France, and so, Wollenberg declared at our table, would Russia. Roth knew that Otto von Hapsburg had offered to lead a legion of Austrian exiles into battle. The world was waiting, holding its breath—and what emerged in this calm before the storm was Chamberlain's last hope: Benito Mussolini. In response to a British plea the Duce had interceded with his German friend and won another day's delay for a new meeting.

To Munich, into the storm clouds, flew the trio of Mussolini, Chamberlain, and Daladier on September 30. We saw them in the newsreel, wearing miens of concern, and no one will ever forget the British prime minister's shielding umbrella. The German generals, medals on their chests, stood behind their Führer and kept quiet.

We too kept quiet. That night nobody was missing at the café. Now and then Roth got up and headed slowly, unsteadily, for the telephone to keep in touch with God and the world; back in his seat he would take a sip and say nothing. "Did you reach anyone?" Mehring asked at last.

Roth raised his glass: "Tomorrow we'll have war." Tomorrow. . . .

Sirens howl somewhere, sometime—yesterday, today, tomorrow? A picture lights up, and I see fists clenched against tank columns in the old streets of Prague, with fingers smearing swastikas on the armor plate. . . . The tanks keep rolling across Wenceslas Square, through an unarmed mass of men and women, workers, students, children. Rocks are thrown; a tank bursts into flames; infantry moves up, goose-stepping.

This is not the Parisian newsreel, and neither is it the Wehrmacht. It is the Red Army conquering Prague thirty years later, the fraternal seizure of Czechoslovakia by troops of the Soviet Union and its four sister republics, and these are the last films taken by Czech newsmen, smuggled out to Vienna, thrown via satellite onto the TV screen in New York, where I sit watching the occupation of Prague. . . . Thirty years in kaleidoscope: from Munich to Moscow. Till the last rock is hurled. . . .

The picture fades. A familiar face takes shape under graying hair, restful in view of ruin. Eric Sevareid gives us his daily comment on the news for C.B.S. Television, and little wrinkles play about the mouth that speaks in a calm, detached voice. The bright eyes are on mine, but he cannot see me. The fronts have shifted, and we are no closer to brotherhood. Is it so wild a dream?

"Don't we know our history too well to have to repeat it?" Carli writes from New Delhi. The public-information officer of the World Health Organization, southeast Asian region, also thinks back thirty years as the Russians occupy Prague. "Again the Czechs. . . ."

Yes, it was our history. "We have sustained a total, unmitigated defeat," Winston Churchill stated in the British House of Commons and had to wait for a storm of protest to subside before he could go on: "All the countries of Mittel Europa and the Danube valley, one after another, will be drawn into the vast system of Nazi politics radiating from Berlin. . . . And do not suppose that this is the end. It is only the beginning."

It was only the beginning. Roth had been mistaken; we did not have war—not yet. We had a pledge of "peace in our time" from Chamberlain, who in turn had Hitler's pledge that Czechoslovakia was his "last territorial demand."

What came next was indeed not territorial, and we did not need the radio to tell us about the pretext. We heard that directly; it happened in Paris, and the news spread like wildfire. At the German Embassy on November 7 a teenage boy demanded to see the ambassador. The third secretary came out instead—and collapsed, shot fatally. The young gunman was only too glad to tell the police that he, Herschel Grynszpan, seventeen, had meant to kill the German envoy because his father had been deported to Poland, along with ten thousand other Polish Jews living in the Reich. Poland had always been an anti-Semitic country; the son may have thought it worse than Nazi Germany. He certainly did not know that his victim, Secretary of Legation Ernst vom Rath, had been under Gestapo surveillance for insufficient anti-Jewish zeal.

The consequence of this murder was the "crystal night," in which synagogues burned down throughout the Reich and not a windowpane was spared in any Jew's home or business. According to the next morning's preliminary Gestapo report to Marshal Göring, "119 synagogues were set on fire, another 76 completely destroyed . . . 815 shops destroyed. . . . 171 residences listed as destroyed indicate only a fraction of the actual damage by arson." In addition, a fine of a billion marks was levied on the victims, payable by all Jews in the Reich, and Adolf Hitler's definition of a Jew went back unto the third and fourth generation.

"Honor thy father and thy mother," I mused aloud, "but woe unto you if they're Jews. . . ."

"That's the stuff we need." It came from across the table, where K.G. had seemed too deep in conversation with Vera to pay attention to anything else. It was amazing how often K.G., who was quite hard of hearing, would hear exactly what he wished to hear.

73

He seemed to live rather poorly in his room in Montparnasse; it was not until later that I got to see his other quarters, where the work was done. He paid well for material he could use. Newday was his liaison with headquarters in London, where the money came from and the texts were printed. They went to Germany on scattered pages of innocent books; my version of the Fourth Commandment was bound in a catechism.

Carli typed the texts. We were a team once again—a lucky break, for the agency business was dwindling: two sales all winter, both to Gallimard. We sold Wollenberg's book about the Red Army, and a novel by Annemarie Selinko, which we handled for the Passer Verlag, of Vienna. Rolf Passer, a Czech citizen, had moved to Prague after the Anschluss and flew to Paris in the new refugee wave after Munich. He joined us at the Hôtel de l'Univers and sought from there to sell his remaining stock of German books while I kept offering translation and movie rights.

Passer found few buyers but many eager listeners. Most of the habitués at Roth's table knew the publisher from Vienna, and all of them wanted to hear about Prague, about the reaction to events. How did the Czechs feel after Munich?

"Sold out," said Passer. He spoke of rage and frustration; of the fists that a national hero, the one-eyed General Jan Sirovy, had clenched behind his back while exhorting Czechs to keep calm; of a government forced to cede its border defenses and to avoid any pretext under which its neighbor might swallow the rest.

No pretext was needed. On March 15, 1939, Adolf Hitler slept in Hradcany Castle and proudly announced after breakfast that Czechoslovakia had ceased to exist. In two days another successor state to the old Danube monarchy had been swallowed, as if to celebrate the anniversary of the Austrian appetizer.

The French and British protests were matters of form. *Why England Slept* was the title of a thesis written then by a

young American student in London; the author's name was
John F. Kennedy. Only Winston Churchill grasped it all:
not just that Hitler was beginning to devour Europe piece
by piece, but what was bitten off now and what was next on
the menu. He saw not just what had happened on the two
Ides of March, 1938 and 1939, but also how it tied in with
events of two decades earlier, of 1918 and 1919. As Sir
Winston put it: "There is not one of the peoples or provinces
that constituted the empire of the Hapsburgs to whom
gaining their independence has not brought the tortures
which ancient poets and theologians had reserved for the
damned."

There came a day, not long after Madrid fell, when we
found Roth sitting as if turned to stone in his chair at the
Café de Tournon. He sat and stared at a newspaper. Mehring
took Carli and me aside. "It's Toller," he whispered. "He
has hanged himself in his New York hotel room." But he
was in America, it ran nonsensically through my mind.

Roth did not notice us any more. He was no longer
writing, only drinking. It was the week before the Whitsun
holiday, and we others decided to get out of Paris for a few
days, to get away from it all. Vera went looking for a job
somewhere; Lajos von Horvath, Passer, Carli, and I went to
the seashore in Normandy. It was too cold for swimming, but
we spent hours walking on the dunes. I looked at the surf, at
the foaming breakers that came over and over, and I heard
Odon: "I love the sea. . . ."

A week after Toller's death I found a note from Mehring
awaiting me at our hotel. Roth had been taken to a hospital,
he wrote, with another attack of delirium tremens; after total
withdrawal of alcohol he had died in a straitjacket on May
27. "It was not an easy death," the letter ended.

We took the next train back but came too late. The mortal
Joseph Roth was in the ground. Vera and I had kept our
word and missed his funeral; now we wished we could tell
him that we hadn't meant to.

Black, wordless, roseless, Manga Bell sat at the silent table. "It must have been Toller's death," Morgenstern would mutter now and then, as if he could not believe it. And Mehring wrote: "Where in the world can you still find a stable of Rightist politics and Left-Kultur, the sort that near the Luxembourg would meet at Joseph Roth's table—who, presage dripping from his every breath, was sage enough to drink himself to death?"

I look back. And the world is very still.

CHAPTER 5

Interlude

I love bridges. Bridges link divided shores; they span the air above a river or gorge or, as in New York, between islands. All around the concrete canyons of Manhattan there are bridges reaching over the arms of the sea, and when fog and smog cover the city, it is hard to see where the metal miracles end. They get lost in the clouds, like the rainbow of which the Bible says that it appeared after the flood to seal God's covenant with earth.

I have always loved bridges. They lead to and fro in space and time. Odon von Horvath wrote a play called *To and Fro;* it is set on a bridge located on a closed border where there is no "to," only "fro," and the play came to my mind on the bridge of Clairac, where the Lot river winds its way to the Garonne, in a part of southern France also known as God's Garden. I used to spend hours on that bridge, just leaning on the rail and looking at the river banks—one steep and defiant, one pleasantly rounded, like different halves of the same face.

The village of Clairac, which the bridge leads into, belongs to the township of Agen. It developed round an abbey in the sixteenth century and grew with the tobacco brought to these parts in the seventeenth by the Mendès family, forebears of Pierre Mendès-France, a politician of the twentieth. The original old stone bridge had just made way for a new metal one in the summer of 1939, when I was marooned in the village—or invited, rather, to vacation there. It was the tobacco that attracted Rolf Passer, my publisher friend who saw no future in books. He had money coming from our sales of translation rights, and he planned to invest it in a farm in southern France. To learn the tobacco-growing art he went to work as a volunteer farmhand for some Czech compatriots who owned a tobacco farm near Clairac. I was to be his guest for two weeks at Clairac's only hotel, Les Glycines.

I too was to look into the situation. Perhaps I could learn to sell tobacco instead of literature or to preside over a chow line, passing out soup to Passer's future hired hands—like Lois Sevareid serving spaghetti from her big bowl, I thought, trying to make the prospect less unattractive.

I was glad to get out of Paris. The table in the café on the Rue de Tournon was forsaken, the Hôtel de l'Univers all but empty, with Lajos gone to his parents, Vera to Spain with a touring theater group, Mehring to Normandy. Clairac seemed paradise, my haven from the flood. Only shadows followed me: Carli promised to keep in touch and to forward material from K.G., Nazi propaganda stuff that might give me ideas for anti-Nazi leaflets. The mail was Clairac's only link with the outside world; the nearest railway station, Tonneins, was five miles away. There Passer met my train and put me on a rented bicycle so I could visit him each afternoon in the tobacco fields of Colleignes, five miles in the other direction.

I would watch him at work or read a new American book I had brought from Paris, a big best-seller called *Gone with the Wind*. It took my mind overseas again, but Passer refused even to dream about America. It was no place for us; competition was too tough, and we'd simply starve over there, he would explain when his aching back forced him to pause in his efforts to plow a straight furrow or when the sun finally set and the oxen had to go back into the barn. Dead tired but contented and looking forward to well-earned sleep, he would bid me good-bye and send me pedaling back to the little town on the Lot in twilight.

I always stopped on the bridge. In the riverbed below, the reeds whispered and the waves rippled around jagged rocks, and as the shadows crept higher, ghosts would emerge from the water—all at once the water would be flowing underneath the Nussdorf Bridge, with the Leopoldsberg rising steeply, defiantly, from the Danube and the pleasantly rounded Kahlenberg next to it, and I would revel in the sight, knowing only too well that it was a mirage. Home was inseparably tied to me but lost forever. I was not traveling; I was in exile. I could not, must not go home again. This was the difference, and it was not to be bridged.

From the carpenter's shop at the end of the bridge I heard hammer blows in time to a gay, singing voice. "*Mon coeur se rappelle. . . .*" I forget the lyrics, except for that one line, but the melody has lingered to this day. Last summer was the first time in thirty years that I stood on the bridge of Clairac again, having motored from Toulouse after flying from New York. One can travel fast nowadays, but at the well by the end of the bridge the women of Clairac still do their washing exactly as they did then. Horvath had also seen women washing—at the village well of Henndorf, near Salzburg—but he used to see them at midnight and say, "They must have plenty of dirt to wash out." If you approached them, the laundresses of Henndorf vanished down the well. . . .

Those of Clairac kept right on working and chatting in

their *patois du Midi* when I passed them again after thirty years. The sun sets behind the vineyards as it always did, but the carpenter's shop at the end of the bridge is closed. In place of the sign "DUBOIS, PÈRE ET FILS," it bears a warning: "NE PAS S'ARRÊTER"—"No stopping."

The road to the hotel where I stayed in 1939 runs uphill through narrow, crooked alleys. The houses looked like witches' cottages then, and through many a dingy window-pane the evil eye was upon me, but I did not care. I knew I was called *l'autrichienne* in the village, like Queen Marie Antoinette in her time, but it took me a while to find out that my head did not sit too securely on my shoulders either.

Today many of the medieval cottages have been modernized, or else they lie in ruins, with only sunflowers looking out the windows. The little square on the hilltop has been built up, and parked outside the old hotel are autos rather than bicycles. I went in, surprised to step into a freshly painted dining room instead of the old bar where the fat *patronne* used to enthrone herself amid bottle towers like the one at the Café de Tournon. Mme. Lacoste, of the Hôtel-Restaurant Les Glycines, rarely rose, for the extrication of her masses of flesh was a complex procedure; reaching the top step with her short legs required the use of the counter top as leverage for her vast bosom. She never got up on my account.

The *patron* used to sit in a corner with a bottle of wine. The pair had grown children, but so far Madame had not brought herself to legalize the relationship. Under French law a husband would become co-owner of the hotel, and Madame was willing to share her life for love's sake, but not her property.

In the kitchen last year I found the new owners, a young couple fresh from Toulouse. They said they were booked up all summer with vacationers from Paris, but this early in the season I could have a room. Once again I filled out a registration blank; under "nationality," instead of "ex-

autrichienne," I wrote "U.S.A." The looks I got were curious but not hostile.

"I was here years ago," I said and asked about Mme. Lacoste. The name meant nothing to the young people. They said the hotel had changed hands several times before, but the bar next door had once belonged to it; I might have better luck there.

I decided to take a stroll first. The old pagan temple on the way to the gendarmerie post is all overgrown now, and in back of the hotel a new tree-lined little street leads to the cemetery. It used to be a forest path. The new street sign says: "Avenue des Déportés."

The barkeeper cannot recall either Mme. Lacoste or the deportations. Both were before his time. Oldsters in the village still talk of the influx in the early 1940's, though, when more and more people came from Bordeaux and Agen and Toulouse to hide out around here. Eventually there were really too many, and one night the gendarmes came, also from Bordeaux and Agen and Toulouse, to round up the fugitives. They were deported, God knows where. Only a few were saved—"by our Resistance," the barkeeper concluded proudly.

That had been after my time; I had left Clairac late in 1939. And I suddenly thought of the name of the aperitif we used to drink then: "Do you have a Claquesin *à l'eau?* "

"*Mais certainement, madame.*"

He turned to the bar. "*Avec citron*," I called after him what I had almost forgotten.

Mon coeur se rappelle—my heart remembers. . . .

The incident began on the bridge. I came bicycling back from the tobacco fields one evening; the vesper bells were tolling, and as the railing I liked to lean on appeared ahead, I saw a young man plunge, fully clothed, into the water. A scream shrilled above the church bells. It came from across the river, where a small crowd stood staring, paralyzed. I stopped on the bridge and stared too. The man came to the surface in midstream, close to the dam, and promptly went down in a whirlpool. I was about to jump after him when he came up again and dived once more, as if looking for something. I got back on my bicycle and raced along the bank, past the laundresses, who dropped their linens and ran after me. "Jeannot! Jeannot," screeched a woman's voice.

Two men were rowing a boat out to the swimmer. He emerged in their path, hair dripping, struggling to lift something. The boat turned, heeling dangerously as the men tried to take in a small body, but just when I thought it would capsize, the man in the water managed to steady it. The body slid into the stern. Slowly, with tired arm-strokes, the swimmer followed the boat ashore.

I stood in the crowd, on tiptoe, watching the child's body laid on the sand. Water and algae ran from the open mouth. A woman threw herself over the child's body; then the crowd drew back to let two gendarmes pass, and I ran away.

Better not get involved, I thought; I don't belong. Hastily I pushed my bicycle uphill, past the well and the carpenter's shop. The door stood open; a dog barked at me. Through empty alleys I got to my hotel.

Inside, arms akimbo, the *patronne* was railing at the *patron*. "Why don't the brats learn to swim?" she yelled at him as if it were his fault. It startled me that she knew; for the first time I saw how fast news travels in a French village.

In the window niche my table was set as usual. Paulette, the waitress, was bustling about, dabbing at reddened eyes that made her look even more like a rabbit. Paulette's upper lip failed to cover her teeth, and her rabbitlike diffidence left her prey to all of the local youth; when her baby was born, they could probably all claim paternity.

They were just pouring through the door. I could never tell them apart; they were all so young. "Paulette," one called from far off, "a round for everybody!"

The rabbit ran. Two eyes like coals caught mine. Where

had I heard that voice? *Quel beau garçon*—where had I seen him? I felt my face flushing; I'd better look away, I thought, but the moment lingered.

"Here's to the rescuer!" chirped another one. A load fell off my mind: The child was alive. Someone filled my glass. The wine sparkled; it was champagne. The black eyes were right in front of me. "*À nos amours*," said the voice, and now I knew it: It came from the carpenter's shop. I looked up, lifting the glass, and saw a high brow between the charcoal eyes and a black mop that was no longer dripping.

"*À vous, Monsieur le Sauveteur*," I replied.

Glasses clinked, black eyes danced. "*Voilà*," the voice exulted; "I've won the bet." A hand touched my arm, making my spine tingle. "*S'il vous plaît, madame*," said the voice cajolingly, "won't you join us?"

All at once I belonged to the circle. Each evening I had been sitting alone in the window niche, my book opened before me like a protective fan. Gone with the Wind. . . . The nearest ones introduced themselves: The thin blond on my right was René, the hairdresser's assistant; the fat one on my left was Gaston, of the garage; the black eyes across the table belonged to Gilbert, the carpenter.

"Monsieur Dubois?" I asked.

"Dubois *fils*," he said gaily. How could I have mixed him up with the rest? None of them looked like Gilbert.

"What was the bet?" I wanted to know. "Who would jump after the child?"

A cork popped. The table guffawed. "*Quelle idée*," exclaimed the rescuer. "By then he'd have drowned. If there had been more time to think, I wouldn't have jumped—I'm a coward. I was looking for you, on the bridge, and so I saw Jeannot chase his balloon right into the water."

The smoke above the table curled into a blue balloon, and the bet, I gathered from the buzz of voices, had concerned me: who would manage to talk to me first. Gaston had been the favorite, since he could offer a ride in his car. "Now he'll pay," said Gilbert and ordered *foie gras,* the specialty of the region.

Armagnac automatically followed the champagne. "*A l'autrichienne de Clairac,*" said Gilbert. "*Je l'aime.*" Clairac or me? My head swam. My cheeks burned. The *patron* in the corner had fallen asleep by his bottle.

Balmy air caressed my hot cheeks as Gilbert escorted me across the hotel yard to the rear entrance of the little inn. My room was up there on the second floor, and in the triangular sky above us the moon hung like a balloon. "*A demain,*" Gilbert said. "Till tomorrow."

Later, in bed, green algae clung to my limbs, dragging me down until two black eyes shone in the water ahead of me. I swam after them as they rose higher and higher in the air that carried me like water, and then a blue balloon appeared ahead, hanging in the air and looking at me out of the shining black eyes, and it was the moon.

At breakfast in my window niche I tried to reconstruct the dream, but the morning sun dissolved it. Gleaming in its rays, instead of a blue balloon, was a white bicycle. A lithe figure dismounted, and bit by bit I recognized the boyish face of yesterday, the high brow, the straight Roman nose. "Come along, 'Ertha," said M. Dubois *fils*—Frenchmen always drop their aitches. "I've closed the shop to show you Clairac."

From that day on I learned to see Clairac through Gilbert's eyes. We climbed the rickety wooden stairs of the bell tower, from which one sees far into Gascony, over hills and castles and over the Lot and the Garonne merging in the valley, all the way to the white-capped chain of the Pyrenees which lines the vault of heaven. Gilbert was singing again: "*Nous sommes les cadets de Gascogne, les cadets de Casteljaloux*"—he looked as if he were the man Cyrano de Bergerac wrote the love letters to Roxanne for; but Gilbert did not know about such literary associations. He pointed out the tall cypress trees one can see scattered all over the landscape, always two by two, growing close together as though from one root, and he explained that they were Huguenot grave markers. Barred from cemeteries, forbidden to lie under crosses, the Huguenots buried their dead in the fields and planted cypress saplings to mark the spots. Clairac was a hotbed of those religious wars; in spite of royal decrees and hangings in the marketplace, the Huguenots would always rise again, and surreptitiously the quarrel was still going on.

"But not for me," said Gilbert. He showed me the old pagan temple, only half overgrown then, and I heard it was "a marvelous love nest." Past a deserted fountain with Renaissance spires—a tourist attraction today—we returned to the bridge we both loved. "But the old one was more beautiful," Gilbert said.

The house with the shop was his family's; for a hundred years the sign had said "DUBOIS, PÈRE ET FILS." "That's Diane," he said when a wagging tail greeted us, and he introduced us: "Diane—'Ertha." Diane had come to him as a starved puppy, but she was a lady now, and when she shook herself, the sawdust flew. It lay ankle-deep around the power saw and the fragrant finished boards stacked against the walls. Innumerable dusty saws and planes hung between the cobwebs on the ceiling.

Gilbert had brought the electric saw from Bordeaux, where he had served his apprenticeship—"*un temps formidable*," he recalled, for the master's wife had introduced him to *l'amour* until the master threw him out. When he came home, his father had wanted to throw out both him and the saw, for Dubois *père* did not hold with such devil's work. He still didn't, although at seventy he now confined himself mostly to bill-collecting, his son said.

High on a wall among the saws and cobwebs I discovered four delicate wooden wheels. Gilbert brought them down for me to look at. They were light as feathers, smooth as glass, and artfully ornamented. One of Gilbert's ancestors had made them for an invention of his, a perpetual-motion machine—if the wheels were flawless, he had thought, there was no reason why they should not turn for eternity. In the end this Great-great-grandfather Dubois had fallen victim to his own inventiveness: Convinced that if birds could fly, so could men, he had built a huge set of wings. One day he had climbed the church spire, strapped on the wings before an astonished crowd, and flown straight into eternity—or rather into the middle of the Lot River.

The bare rectangular box between the unfinished pieces of furniture was going to be a coffin, Gilbert explained. All you had to do there was to nail some boards together—what else does one need when he's dead? Some people wanted a crucifix on the lid. "It's good business."

Next to the coffin stood a cradle. This Gilbert had artfully carved, free of charge, for his sister's first-born. Unfortunately Janine had not wanted it; her husband was a silk manufacturer and liked modern things only. "I like all things here," Gilbert said. "Not the work especially; no one in Clairac likes work. But when I've made enough money, I simply close down. I'm my own master. It's a wonderful life."

I regarded him almost with envy. How good to live like that, between cradle and coffin—like Hans the Lucky in Grimm's fairy tale or Jean de la Lune in the French song, rather—and how much fun one could have here!

The nearest movie house was in Tonneins, but there was dancing in Clairac at the beach restaurant. Before taking me there, Gilbert found it necessary to warn me of his bad reputation in the village: almost thirty and still unmarried! People said he ought to hurry up. "But I have plenty of time," he said, and I thought: It's good I haven't.

His next warning concerned me. The villagers—not he,

of course—knew hardly any foreigners and disliked refugees in particular. When the hordes of fugitives from Spain had come and been put into camps, he personally had given asylum to one of them. A charming woman; her husband had been killed in the civil war over there. Later she had been expelled from France and had gone all the way to Russia. She was still writing letters from there now and then, which always arrived open—the postmistress was jealous, Gilbert explained. "But no one here can read them anyway. We speak some Basque, but no Spanish." Asked how he himself had communicated with the Spanish woman, he merely smiled.

In the evening, when I returned from the tobacco fields, we went to the beach on the river—"the unique beach," the signs called it. Located below the dam, it was ringed by old trees and had a terrace restaurant facing the narrow strip of sand. Today the beach is a camping ground, restaurant and trees are gone, and a new power plant keeps floodlights burning, but thirty years ago it was dark under the trees. In the foliage Chinese lanterns shimmered like glowworms, and roundabout the moon one could see the stars. "They'll still hang high when we're laid low," Horvath had written.

"Mon coeur se rappelle. . . ." The record was cracked from much use: *"Rappelle—rappelle,"* it kept repeating till someone would nudge the needle. We danced under the Chinese lanterns, René and the rabbit, Gaston and the postmistress, Gilbert and I. While the records were being changed, we took a few sips at the table; the local wine tasted to me like a Vienna *heuriger. "Parlez-moi d'amour,"* began the next record.

Gilbert took my arm. "You belong to us now."

"Et malgré moi je veux y croire," the record sang. We danced the side, and then the other side: *"J'attendrai. . . ."* At dawn, I knew, everything would dissolve like the mirage of the Vienna Woods on the bridge.

At dawn we stood before my door. "I'll come with you,"

Gilbert stated as a matter of course. I slapped his face, and his eyes danced as if he had won another bet.

Upstairs, peering cautiously out of the window, I saw him lean like a shadow against the moonlit courtyard wall, and like the voice of the wind it rang up to me. "*J'attendrai. . . .*"

Friend Rolf Passer took a day off too to show me something. We were to inspect an agricultural emigré colony in the vicinity. At times when his resolve to buy a farm would waver, shaken by the threat of war, Passer considered settling among these fellow refugees. One of them was an editor he knew from Prague.

We lost our way in the rolling hill country that did remind me of the Vienna Woods, and a peasant we met behind his swaying two-wheeled ox cart shook his head, baffled, when asked for directions to the farm cooperative at the location Passer had in his address book. "The place with the foreigners," I said at last, and the man nodded and raised his stick to point the way uphill.

Having pushed our bicycles to the hilltop, we beheld a number of identical little huts set in rows at exactly equal distances from one another. They had thatched roofs, no fences, and sheep and goats grazing peaceably in between. "Idyllic!" Rolf exclaimed.

The property had been leased for a nominal sum to the emigrés by a committee that also supplied them with farm machinery and animals. Goats and sheep, Passer knew, were particularly inexpensive in their upkeep. The sheep bleated, and we knocked on the first hut. A young man answered; when Passer asked for his friend Hanusch, the young man introduced himself as Hanusch's assistant, Huber, from Vienna, and invited us to step in. The hut was furnished with packing crates and decorated with abstract paintings, for Huber had been an artist at home, not a farmer. "And what do you do here?" Rolf inquired.

"Nothing much," Huber said happily. His two employers, Dr. Hanusch, the ex-editor from Prague, and Dr. Mayer, formerly a physician in Berlin, were still arguing about where to begin.

"Someone ought to take charge," Passer suggested.

The young man shook his head. "The totalitarian principle won't work here. On account of the books."

I liked that. "What books?"

Hanusch's agricultural dictionary and Mayer's pharmaceutical one, it seemed. Mayer wanted to make chemical fodder, not just chemical fertilizer like Hanusch, and when the cute little rabbits died, Hanusch had accused Mayer of killing them. Huber thought it had been an accident, rather like the subsequent one when Hanusch's cat ate Mayer's chickens, leaving the cock a widower.

Rolf decided to act as peace-maker. We went to look for Hanusch and found him cutting a trail with the committee's new tractor. After a cordial hello Rolf began to advise him on tractor operations, and I went back to the hut because dark clouds were gathering and I smelled the aroma of a pot of coffee that Huber had brewed in the meantime.

A thunderclap interrupted our first cup. Had the storm broken? Through the window I saw a bearded, bespectacled head stuck out of the next hut—Dr. Mayer's, evidently. Huber shot past me; I saw wisps of smoke drift through the open door. "It's nothing," Huber called from outside. "Just the tractor blew up."

I ran out behind the bearded neighbor. Huber stood protectively in front of me as Mayer and Hanusch advanced against Passer from two sides: "Our tractor," they yelled in unison. "He's ruined it!"

The first drops fell as Rolf and I took rapid leave from the cooperative enterprise. The thunderstorms of the Midi suit the temper of its inhabitants: They break violently and pass swiftly. Torrents of water rushing down the road drove us to seek shelter under a tree, and amid lightning and thunder I could not hold back a comment on the experience.

"Idyllic, eh?" I said—and then lightning struck between us. We fought until the air cleared and the roads were dry enough to pedal back.

Sopping wet, we arrived at the hotel, and there, playing cards with his *copains*, was Gilbert. He got up to greet us, shook hands warmly with Passer, and invited him to join the game, but Rolf said he had to get home and into dry clothes. "You running around with the village boys would be the last straw," Rolf told me at the door.

The next day I told Gilbert I did not want to go dancing. "Good," he said in agreement. "We'll take a boat ride."

The boat, the broad, flat-bottomed one by which the boy Jeannot had been rescued, was down by the beach now. Gilbert rowed it halfway across the Lot; then we drifted downstream. Dance music rang after us: "*Je t'aime—quand-même. . . .*" There was no crack in this record; Gilbert had brought it to the restaurant for me. Frogs were croaking somewhere, and two moons shone, a balloonlike one in the sky and one in the water, drifting alongside. I trailed my hand in the silvery flow that was tepid and soft like the air, and like a lullaby Gilbert sang, "*Jean de la lune. . . .*"

That's you, I thought. The music stopped; the boat swayed; suddenly Gilbert was next to me, and we sat steadying each other, drifting into the dark, close, not moving. Any move would have upset the boat's balance. He did not even try to kiss me, to my regret.

"Isn't it nice to be in love?" he asked.

"Do you tell that to every woman you get into a boat?"

"No. Only if it's true."

I must not fall in love, I thought. "We're drifting too far," I said.

Willow branches caressed the waves from the bank; he reached for one and pulled us ashore. He tied the boat to a gleaming willow trunk and lifted me out. A nightingale sang—there are many thereabouts. The air was dry; I felt parched all of a sudden. "Let's take a dip," I proposed.

I shouldn't have done that. In two winks Gilbert was out of his clothes, facing me, stark naked. *Quel beau garçon.* . . . I don't like the looks of naked men as a rule, but with him I liked everything. *"Et vous?"* he asked.

"It's too light," I said, embarrassed. There are two kinds of women, a man once told me: those who make love with the light on and those who turn it off—"like you," he added. He was so right that I told him to get out and stay out.

Gilbert laughed, pointing at the moon that hid behind a cloud. "The fool won't watch."

I laughed, slipped out of my clothes, and plunged into the water, Gilbert on my heels. We played tag, dived through the swirling waves, swam up and down and across the river with Gilbert above me, below me, until he caught me and carried me ashore in his arms as if I had no weight at all. I lay stretched out in the grass, on the scented earth, and he knelt above me. *"Je t'aime—que faire?"*

Just play, I was wishing, just play. . . .

Like willow branches caressing the waves, cool hands made of air are playing with me. . . . The Lot, the landscape, the moon, are just background. . . . My skin feels cool. . . . Only where the fingers touch me it begins to burn underneath. . . . Flames are licking upward from my breasts. . . . Flames are being sucked in by kisses, deeper and deeper inside me. . . . I'm going up in flames. . . . my body is burning. . . . a river is sweeping us along. . . . I'm swimming off in its waves . . . being whirled high into the air . . . melting in the moonlight. . . .

"Chérie, tu reviens d'un joli petit voyage," a voice says.

I return to earth. . . .

"Vois donc, ton jou-jou, your toy—it's waking me up again."

"Vois donc, chérie—look, a lifetime isn't enough for how much I want you."

I look up. "Tomorrow it must be all over."

"Tomorrow?" Gilbert repeats. "What's that?"
And we fall back into the night. . . .

"Do you hear what the Lot says?" Gilbert asked at
dawn, when we stood on the bridge again. He bent over
the railing, listening. "You must stay with us—"

The small waves murmured, enveloped the sharp rocks
that sought to hold them, and continued, hissing, toward the
sea. The sea comes with new waves, over and over again—
I'd like to see it again myself, I thought. I could never stay
here. I had lost myself on this nocturnal trip to the moon—
lost myself, my body and my mind. Moments between heaven
and earth do not last.

"Don't think, *chérie*," Gilbert said. "Then you can't hear
the voices." He could hear them; he lived them. To bring
the unconscious to consciousness had been the goal of
Horvath's writing. *Les extrèmes se touchent.*

"You don't love me," Gilbert said gently. *"C'est seulement
le béguin."* Only *le béguin*—what did that mean? I did not
know the word; it must be a local idiom. I could never find
the right translation. "Something that dies quickly," a
Frenchwoman told me. A crush, I told myself.

"Tonight at the hotel," Gilbert and I agreed, parting on the
bridge.

Waiting at the post office was a letter from Carli. The
postmistress gave it to me open, with an icy look, and I beat
a hasty retreat; luckily there was no Nazi material in the
envelope. Or had it been removed? What Carli wrote seemed
harmless: some general things about the worsening Polish
crisis and a reminder that I ought to return to Paris soon—
there was work to be done. Or should he come and get me, to
be on the safe side?

On the safe side? There was no such thing anymore. Even
Passer agreed with me there. Since the mishap at the cooperative idyll he had abandoned all hope of interesting me in
agriculture. At the moment, he said, it was impossible to

make decisions anyway; in case of war, he, as a lieutenant in the Czechoslovak Army Reserve, would immediately report for duty to the Czech government in exile. In the meantime one just had to wait as calmly as possible.

"Wait just ten minutes," Gilbert asked me that night at the hotel. There was a trifling matter to be settled; he would be back on the dot. The trifle was an unimportant affair with a woman friend who had just come back from vacation. "In ten minutes I'll be done," Gilbert vowed and left.

I put a sheet of paper on the table to write to Carli and answer that I was coming. The clock on the far wall distracted me; it kept ticking and ticking, but the hands seemed to stand still. Instead of writing, I began to stare at them: They did move, but infinitely slowly. . . . Seven minutes . . . Eight . . . nine. . . . My sheet of paper remained blank. After thirty years I still see the face of that grandfather clock before me. That's over, I thought. At ten I'll run away. . . . Then Gilbert came through the door.

"Done," he called merrily. "Let's celebrate at the barbecue." And in another minute we were rolling out of Clairac in Gaston's car, past the cemetery, on the rutted forest road since renamed Avenue des Déportés.

"What did you tell the lady?" I asked.

"Yvonne?" He shrugged. Something. He wasn't a fanatic for the truth.

This was how Odon used to talk. Looking at Gilbert, from the side in particular, I was sometimes struck by a resemblance to Horvath's profile. And I'd tell myself to watch out; I was beginning to imagine things.

The whole thing with Yvonne had been silly, Gilbert explained; she merely wanted an occasional diversion when her husband was on night duty—he was the chief of gendarmes. This frightened me, but Gilbert saw nothing to worry about. Yvonne couldn't talk, so she couldn't harm us; it was as simple as that, he told me gaily, driving through the woods. I hoped he was right.

Some Roman ruins huddled eerily by the roadside, and then a clearing opened in the woods. A fire burned in front of an old farmhouse between ancient trees, ringed by a circle of shadowy figures. Only one bearded, aquiline face was brightly lit by the flames, for the man held the spit on which a pig was slowly turning.

His name was Noguès. He owned this wilderness farm and was never called by his first name like the rest. I did not know any of them; they had come from various places in the region, some from as far as Toulouse. The only other girl was a dark, vivacious one named Mara, who came over to sit with me. Gilbert and she were the children of neighbors, she said, and she had a factory job in Toulouse now. Her tiny car stood next to ours.

With the roast pig, wine was flowing like water from a keg. When the fire had burned down and the forest air got chillier, we went on drinking indoors, where there were all kinds of tools and tackle but not enough chairs; the young fellows sat around the floor, Mara on somebody's lap. Gilbert showed me the shelves on the wall, shelves that ran up to the heavy beams of the ceiling, and I was surprised to see them filled from top to bottom with books. Trying to make out some of the titles in the semidarkness, I was even more surprised. Proudhon, I read—Stirner—Bakunin—Kropotkin—

"*Voilà ma bibliothèque anarchiste.*" Our bearded host had joined us. He had collected the precious volumes himself, he proudly told me, and had read each one. The taciturn man began to talk all of a sudden about living alone in the forest with his animals and books—they were his world, a free, peaceful world without government. Governments, whatever their professed purposes, were institutions of collective violence. They coerced the individual and then, inevitably, one another. The consequence of government was war. By the way, had we heard of Joseph Stalin's pact with Adolf Hitler?

First I thought this was a hoax. It was a trick, said one of the men from Toulouse. Not to be taken seriously, said another. I hated tricks—but they were already talking of something else.

Noguès knew plenty, Gilbert told me on the ride back, and not just from books; he was in touch with informed people in Toulouse. (And after France fell, it was Noguès who organized the resistance of *les maquis*, the "underbrush men," in the Clairac region.)

As for me, my mind was made up after the barbecue. I had to get away, back to my own people. In Paris I could work and be independent. Gilbert mustn't know, or he would not let me leave.

My hurry was so great that, instead of writing, I sent Carli a telegram. It would attract too much attention if he came and got me, but I did want to see him alone first to talk things over. I thought I could afford a little detour. I love the sea; I did not want to leave the lovely Gascon country without having seen the highest dunes in the world. Carli should meet me at the post office in Arcachon, I wired, or send word to me there.

Carrying my small suitcase, I got on my bicycle, earlier in the day than usual, to bid Passer good-bye and take a bus directly from the tobacco fields of Colleignes to the Tonneins railway station.

A couple of days by the sea would do me good, Rolf thought, but I ought to come back shortly, before the harvest in any case. "And in case of war at once," he said as he brought me to the station and bought a return ticket for me. He could not wait for the train, or he would miss the last bus back from Tonneins to Colleignes.

The train from Toulouse was late. When it came at last, I got on, hesitantly fingering my return ticket, wondering whether to tear it up, perhaps, lest I be tempted to use it. I mustn't see Gilbert again, I thought, or I'll never get away.

My God, what's to come out of it? I can't turn into a French peasant girl. I've had my fling—*le béguin*—and it was wonderful, unique, unforgettable.

Absently I put both tickets, *aller* and *retour*, into my pocketbook. Absently I looked through the compartment window at passing telegraph poles. The tracks ran parallel to a highway on which a motorcycle was racing the train. The rider was gaining on us. He sat hunched too low over the handlebars for me to see his face; all I saw was black hair flying in the wind. Gilbert, I thought and shut my eyes. This was going too far. I mustn't fancy every man as Gilbert.

The train stopped at a small Gascon town. "*Chérie*," I heard. Gilbert, all out of breath, waved to me from the platform: "*Chérie*—hand me your suitcase and come."

The suitcase fitted between us on the motorcycle. The train went on, and so did we, in the other direction. "I know a charming little inn here," Gilbert said.

The motorcycle stayed outside; we went in. He took a room, a cozy one with bright pillows on the double bed. "I'm hungry," I said to gain time.

In the dining room we ordered oysters from Arcachon. Nothing in my life had ever tasted better; our plates were piled high with shells when I said I wanted to have a look at the town first. I have forgotten the name of it. I remember only that there was a bridge there too, leading across the Garonne to wide-open fields.

The moon was full that night at the end of August, and there wasn't a soul in sight. We sat on a bench under trees somewhere in the world, alone at last, and when we tired, we lay down in the grass.

The break of dawn found us refreshed and wide awake; only the moon looked pale on the horizon and in need of sleep. Arms around each other, we wandered home. The room lay in twilight behind blue curtains, the pillows strewn in a corner. The bed was still open. I got in. So did Gilbert.

Indiscreet rays of sunlight pierced the curtains, playing on the white sheets, before I realized how late it was. *"Chérie,"* Gilbert said, surprised, "we can make love in bed too. . . . "

We rang for the maid, who brought us coffee and fragrant croissants and, as a special favor, the morning paper from Bordeaux. "HITLER'S LAST TERRITORIAL DEMAND," said the headline. It sounded familiar, but suddenly I realized what was at stake. "Gilbert—you'll be called up!"

He shook his head. *"Ça non*—not under any circumstances. I love life too much." And once again he kissed me from top to toe.

"There's one thing you mustn't do to me, *chérie,"* he said at the station. "You must not go on to Paris without seeing me again."

The train pulled out; we had come to the last moment. *"Au revoir,"* it rang after me, over and over. *"Au revoir. . . ."*

CHAPTER 6

Dossier d'Amour

In Bordeaux I had to change trains, and when I got to Arcachon in the evening, I found a closed post office and no Carli. Helplessly I walked the streets between the luxury hotels and the casino, among fashionably dressed crowds chattering in many languages to the strains of music from the international hit parade. Hitler's advent had changed nothing here. These resorts are all alike the world over, and so are the tunes that pursue you for blocks from the inevitable bandstand.

During one of the welcome pauses something caught my ear. It was just a faint whistle—someone was whistling an old Viennese song we loved, Carli and I. I started running, anxious to trace the sound before the band blared again, and at the next corner there was Carli. "Late as usual," he called, visibly cheered up by my appearance. "I've been whistling for you ever since yesterday."

In harmony we proceeded to the hotel where he had reserved a room for me, a little one on the top floor; and from
my window, across a boat channel and a narrow sand spit,
I could look out on the ocean. I saw the whitecaps rolling
in from the Bay of Biscay, surging, breaking, somersault-
ing, a perpetual-motion machine that wasn't man-made.
"Well, this is it," said Carli.

I meant the sea; he meant the war. Since the Hitler-Stalin
pact our friends in Paris considered it unavoidable. The pact
had split the emigrés; there were fierce fights between those
who feared it would help Hitler's aggression and those who
had it on the highest authority that what looked like help was
really hindrance.

"A trick," I said, quoting the diagnosis made at the barbecue by the men from "Red Toulouse." K.G. called it a
catastrophe, said Carli. Mehring had ridiculed the odd alliance
in a poem for a Paris refugee paper. Even some prominent
Communists from Austria and Germany had signed a mani-
festo against the pact—and would pay with their lives
later.

"And to this Donnybrook I'm to go back?" I asked Carli.

"You're one of us," he replied. "You can't stay in your
witches' coven." We laughed; my letters had given him a vivid
picture of Clairac and the residents of the old houses in its
crooked alleys.

He had new material from K.G. along, but that could wait
till tomorrow. The beach restaurant where we dined faced on
Le Bassin, the natural harbor that looked like a huge pond;
there were Chinese lanterns here too, but they were fakes,
with electric bulbs inside the colored paper, and the music
came out of loudspeakers, and the dancing couples wore
tuxedos and evening gowns. We sat quietly in a corner. I
was very tired. Between a tango and a Lambeth walk a new
appeal from President Franklin D. Roosevelt to Hitler was
read over the radio, and that too had a familiar ring. The bill
was out of proportion with what we had eaten and drunk;

100

the extra charge, evidently, was for the surroundings. We paid and left.

In the morning the beach was so crowded we could hardly find a place to sit. It was high tide, and we swam out as far as we could; when we came back, the tide had turned and left the sand strewn with jellyfish and other sea monsters. Pale-hued, transparent like glass, they were congealing in the sun now, and the dirty seaweed between them exuded a musty smell.

At low tide we worked. I looked through K.G.'s material, at the swastika-crowned announcements of the pact that would now stand rocklike, ironclad, unbreakable, for a decade. Carli told me that K.G.'s own propaganda texts were printed in Paris now, in a print shop in which he himself was working—secretly, because he had no French *permis de travail.*

I made a note of an idea that had occurred to me. "First *against* the Russians," I jotted down, "now *for* the Russians —what do I tell my sons?" Signed: "A German mother." Carli liked the text, and I gave it to him for K.G. to use.

He gave it back. "Go bring your brave German mother yourself," he told me. We never used the word "brave" in the old sense of "valorous" nor in the modern German sense of "upright"; we meant it ironically. "A brave pimp," Horvath liked to say.

The idea went into my suitcase with the Nazi material. On the next day, the last of August, the hotel lobby was full of luggage not only because vacations were at an end but also because the threat of war made many guests leave early. "Just another false alarm like last year," the desk clerk reassured us. "There'll be peace if the Poles accept Monsieur Hitler's terms. They'll give in like the Czechs."

The radio was silent—not broadcasting, or perhaps the clerk had turned it off. The newsstands were sold out. The beach, jam-packed only yesterday, was half empty; we saw crowds heading for the railroad station. We headed the other way, lured south of the beach by the Dune de Playa, nearest of the mountainous, broad, high, empty bulwarks that the sea had thrown up here against itself; and we climbed through the hot sand until Arcachon with its casino, its hotels, its brightly colored villas, lay at our feet like a toy town. Greeting us on our return was the news that Poland had rejected Hitler's demands.

The first of September found us still in Arcachon. I could not make up my mind to return to Paris; Carli did not want to leave alone. The beach lay deserted. The motorboats that take you out to the world's greatest oyster beds rocked sadly by the pier, pennants drooping. "Only four francs today for the round trip," called a young boatman. "Last chance to see the world's finest oysters! Only three francs!"

We got aboard. Beach, hotels, newsstands, radio sets, remained behind. The boat veered toward the narrow pass leading to the open sea; I caught a glimpse of the surf, a tremulous white line, and at the same time the boatman pointed to the right: "*Voilà.*" There, protected by the cape, were the giant oyster beds. It takes three years to raise these oysters and three hours to view them, said the boatman.

We did not have that much time today—would he take us where we could walk briefly across the sand spit? The boatman was willing; he lived out here on Cap Ferret, he said as we approached the jetty at a little fishing village.

And then, behind the last clumps of dune grass, there was the free, endless expanse of beach again, with nothing far and wide except the waves that come rolling in over and over. The tide was rising, and the minutes trickled away with the foam of the surf. We ran into the water, out again, in again. I forgot to take off my wristwatch; the hands stopped, but the breakers went on keeping perfect time. We cheated time with the tide.

Back at the landing, instead of our young boatman, an old woman met us. She wept. What had happened? She told us that the Germans had invaded Poland and her son had been ordered to Bordeaux at once for induction into the army.

"His father was killed in the last war. Just before he was born. Always the *boches!* Don't they have mothers?" sobbed the woman. Her son had taken his boat back with him; we would have to wait for the steamer to Arcachon. It was due in a couple of hours.

We landed among luggage piles in a milling host of inductees, refugees, homebound vacationers. At the post office there were long lines before each window. Long-distance calls were not accepted for the time being; telegrams would be delayed pending the arrival of censorship regulations. No one knew what to do, not even our hotel clerk. According to the radio, he said, the regular trains were supposed to be still running tonight. He had the radio turned on; the melodious time signal rang like a sneer.

We packed, paid, and hurried to the station—just in time to see the train to Bordeaux pull out. It was the price of our stolen hours by the sea, but now we had time aplenty. Carli got in line to buy me a ticket to Paris. "Throw the other one away," he said when he brought it, but I carefully put the new ticket into my pocketbook with the return ticket Passer had already given me.

There was one more train to Bordeaux, but it had no direct connection to Paris. Night had fallen by the time we reached Bordeaux, and the station where we had to wait was pitch-dark except for a few blue lights; blackout orders were in effect, we were told. We found the night train to Paris with some difficulty; it was due to leave at 22:20. On the adjoining track another train was waiting, due to leave at the same time but in the opposite direction, for Toulouse. "Via Tonneins," I said.

Carli took my arm. "You're coming with me."

I did not move. "*Au revoir.*" It rang in my ears. "There's one thing you mustn't do to me, *chérie. . . .*"

103

We stood on the platform between the two trains, Carli and I. Two conductors yelled, "All aboard!" Two whistles shrilled.

I grabbed my suitcase, shouted, "I'll follow you," and ran —away from Carli to board the train to Toulouse.

We left on the minute, in opposite directions. It doubled the speed with which we passed, trying to wave to each other through the windows. With a helpless gesture, as in Vienna only a year before, I saw Carli disappear.

The conductor drew the shade over my window; not a glimmer of light must show. I gave him my ticket without looking, and he returned it with the words, "The Paris train is pulling out over there." Then I found the right ticket, which he took. "Tonneins," he said. "Yes, it's safer in the country."

I wished I could reverse the rumbling wheels, but it was too late. Too late for everything. There was no road back, and Gilbert would be gone anyway. The wheels rumbled on and on. I rode into the night, alone; even the conductor had gone into the next car. There was no deciphering the names of the stations we stopped at; I could only count them, and when I finally got off, I was sure I had counted wrong. It was a dark, strange void in which I stood with my suitcase as the train rolled on.

A gleam approached me through the darkness. It was a bicycle lamp. A shadowy figure dismounted, said, "*Chérie. . . .*" The tears that ran down my face tasted salty, like sea water. On the handlebars of his white bicycle, the way one carries a child at times, Gilbert took me home along the banks of the Lot.

"How did you happen to be there?" I asked.

Simple, he said: Since yesterday he had been meeting every train from Bordeaux.

The Hôtel Les Glycines was long asleep when we arrived,

but Gilbert had a key, and also one to open my room. "We can both report tomorrow," he said.

The night was ours still.

In the morning the wide-open doors of the Clairac town hall were covered with large official announcements. The right-hand ones referred to persons liable to military service, the left-hand ones to "German Matters"—"*Ressortissements Allemandes*." Those concerned either way had to report at once to the authorities.

There was a crowd around the posters, pushing to see who was or was not concerned. A path opened when we approached; men drew back as if they wanted to have nothing to do with us. We went in, but Gilbert was sent right out again: His class wasn't due yet, the clerk said.

Me the clerk kept. With a disapproving glance he asked for my papers. My Parisian *permis de séjour* elicited a snarl: "Why no *carte d'identité?*"

I tried to explain that all refugees such as me had received these temporary permits, valid throughout France, but the explanation seemed to make him only more suspicious. He scrutinized the paper, word by word, and suddenly discovered something. "Who put in this 'ex' before *'autrichienne'?* In different ink?" he added on a note of triumph.

"The prefecture in Paris, after the Anschluss," I said quickly.

The clerk's moustache bristled. He stared at the document and then at me. "I do not see an official stamp," he declared. "Something is wrong here. *Vous êtes allemande.*"

"*Ça non,*" I cried. "Not even Hitler managed to make a German of me!" He asked what I was doing in Clairac, and I replied that I had come down on vacation and would now return to Paris.

"*Ah, ça.*" He shrugged. There were new regulations in force now. "*On verra*—we'll see. You're not *en règle.*" He disappeared with the papers that were not in order, leaving me to wait on a wooden bench.

After a while he returned with the mayor. This rotund, amiable man assured me that I was not under his jurisdiction. Mine was a case for the gendarmerie, to which his clerk would now escort me. We set out, curiously eyed by the crowd outside, and with the clerk carrying not just my little permit but also a fat file. It was my first inkling of the fact that I already had a dossier in Clairac.

The gendarmes, clothed in new uniforms, received us with military salutes. Their chief jovially slapped my escort's back. "It won't be long before you too will wear a uniform, old chap," he said, and the clerk grew visibly paler.

"Now about you, madame," said Chief Lefèbvre with a look that made my heart sink; it was his wife, after all, with whom Gilbert had settled "in ten minutes flat" before taking me to the barbecue. Hell hath no fury. . . . But the chief said only that my case would be investigated and I would remain under surveillance. For the moment that was all. I was free to go.

Through the window I saw Gilbert pace up and down in the street like a sentry. When I emerged, he came running. He tried to joke. "I thought they'd keep you right there."

"So did I," I whispered as we walked to the hotel, trailed at some distance by a pair of gendarmes.

In the afternoon he pedaled to Colleignes in my stead to inform Passer; I did not dare leave the village, with the gendarmes following my every step. When Gilbert returned, Rolf was with him, all set to go to the police and vouch for me. His statement probably served to fatten my file; he himself was on his way to Paris to volunteer for the Czech Army that was being mobilized in France. "They need me, and here there's nothing for me to do," he said, glowering at the gendarmerie post. "If they had given me the *sauf-conduit* for you, you'd have to come along now, like it or not."

The "safe conduct," without which we refugees were now

forbidden to travel, meant not only that you could take a certain trip within a certain time but also that you had to. Rolf's request had been denied out of hand, though, and so, like it or not, I had to stay. I gave him greetings for our friends in Paris; he gave me money to tide me over the time I might be stuck in Clairac, and he promised to write from wherever the tides of war carried him. He kept his promise; that this also helped to keep me stuck, without his meaning it to, I found out much later. He left on September 2, when war had not yet been declared but France and Britain had answered the attack on Poland with an ultimatum.

On the third Gilbert was called for his preinduction physical. The gendarmes no longer let us out of their sight; in the afternoon, when I was waiting in the hotel bar, Chief Lefèbvre himself dropped in to keep an eye on me. His wife sat in a circle of chattering ladies between his table and the vacant one once occupied by the local youths. The ladies—waiting too, I suppose—acted as if I did not exist; only Mme. Jacob, whose little son Gilbert had pulled out of the river, gave me a nod when nobody was looking.

Then the radio announced that England had declared war. It quoted a statement that Prime Minister Neville Chamberlain had broadcast over the B.B.C.: "This is a sad day for all of us, and to none is it sadder than to me. Everything that I have worked for . . . has crashed into ruins."

And France, we thought, what about France? The ladies screeched like angry seagulls. *"Toujours les anglais . . .* it's always the British who're dragging us into war. Who wants to die for the Poles?"

Some of the young men arrived and joined the ladies. Paulette ran to serve them and to get the latest news. Gilbert came in last and joined me. "Turned down," he whispered before calling for wine.

"How did you manage it?" I asked when Paulette was out of earshot.

He shrugged. Had I never noticed that his left leg was a

107

little shorter than the right one? I had not, not even while dancing. "It's my good luck," Gilbert said. "Otherwise I might have had to let the ax slip on purpose."

René came over; he and Gaston had been taken. They envied Gilbert. Gaston was laying bets about me again, and this time the ladies were getting into the act: Was I a spy— yes or no? René and I had to hold onto Gilbert, who wanted to jump Gaston, to kill him. . . . Then the two of us were alone again, with a bottle of wine.

I made up my mind not to drink too much so I wouldn't talk too much. I tried to explain the situation, to make Gilbert understand which side I was on: "We should have fought in Austria," I told him.

He shook his head. "War never helps. Revolution, maybe." It was the French way of thinking. "They can't hurt us here," he said to comfort me.

By then he knew a good deal about me and my friends— except for K.G., of course, whom I never mentioned—but understanding the Nazis was beyond him. The thing about the Jews, he thought, was like that with the Huguenots in Clairac, long, long ago. He did not know any Jews. "What about Léon Blum?" I asked, for he often talked approvingly of the French ex-premier.

Gilbert had to laugh. Léon Blum, he said, was a Socialist, not a Jew—Jews were people like the peddlers who some- times came to sell their junk in the village. Once there had been a woman with them; he remembered her well (*"Elle était charmante"*), and she had broadened his knowledge of the Jews by telling him that her menfolk didn't kiss the way he did. He raised his glass, beaming, and brought me back to the subject. *"À nos amours!"*

Suddenly we saw everyone standing. The radio blared the "Marseillaise": France had declared war. After the last chord a menacing Chief Lefèbvre strode over to us. "You're cele- brating the war?"

"*Fichez nous la paix*—leave us in peace," Gilbert said, unflustered. For the moment it helped.

"Don't be afraid," he whispered at dawn in my room, and I held him tighter when the knocks on the door were repeated.

"Open up!" someone shouted.

"*Un moment, s'il vous plaît*," I called back.

We got out of bed without a sound. Gilbert opened the faucet over the washbasin; with the water running, one could not hear him dress. "Drop these after me, please," he whispered, handing me his shoes. Barefoot, he leaped onto the windowsill and climbed out through the curtains while I wrapped his shoes in an old newspaper. I turned the water off and heard the padding of feet on the roof and then a soft whistle from below. Carefully I dropped the shoes out the window.

The door was being rattled. "Hurry up!"

"I'll be dressed in a second," I replied, my courage rising. I opened and found myself between two gendarmes, who marched me straight to the police station. A large black car was parked outside. Inside, Chief Lefèbvre met us with a gentleman in mufti: an inspector from the Sûreté in Toulouse, come especially for me. My file lay on the desk; my fingerprints were taken; the interrogation reminded me of the Gestapo. Why had I left Germany? What was I doing here? What were my sources of income? Oh, a literary agency—so I had contacts abroad?

The inspector examined my *permis de séjour* with a magnifying glass. "About to expire," he commented, but then he found the stamp beside the "ex"; it had merely slipped a little. The document was put next to the fingerprints for further study, and we moved on to a new section of my dossier: evidence given against me by prominent ladies of Clairac.

Mme. Lacoste, mine hostess, had pointed out suspicious links with a foreigner from the vicinity and a villager of questionable reputation. Neighbors of M. Dubois had counted the hours I spent in observation of the bridge—obviously for espionage purposes—and in reconnoitering hiding places. The inspector took up the next statement, then laid it aside with a glance at Chief Lefèbvre; Yvonne, I thought. The widowed Mme. Irène Duval, postmistress, had confiscated my suspicious correspondence, including letters from abroad as well as a money order from Paris that bore only two letters instead of the sender's name.

"Spies are shot here," the inspector broke into my tangled explanation. He got up. "Come along."

I froze. "Where?"

"First to the hotel, to search your things."

The suitcase, I thought, walking after him—I had unpacked everything but the Nazi stuff. . . .

"Watch it!" someone shouted in the bar as we came in. Young men jumped off tables and chairs, revealing Gilbert and Gaston in the center, and I thought I saw two knives disappear, too fast for anyone to be sure what had happened.

The gendarmes held me; the young men ran. In my room the door was locked behind us and every drawer ripped out and emptied on the floor; in a moment the room looked like the train compartment at the Austrian-Swiss border. The walls seemed to be swaying, and I was allowed to sit down. Then Mme. Jacob came in and sat next to me as if I did not exist; the inspector gave her papers from my file. I understood: She had been summoned as a translator because she came from Alsace and knew some German.

First, a German telegram. It had arrived, via Paris, from a Swedish publisher who expressed interest in the rights to my Suttner biography. What did that mean? I explained that it concerned an old book that the Nazis had banned, the story of an Austrian pacifist.

"In these times you make pacifist propaganda?"

I fell silent. I was not told the date of the telegram Carli had forwarded. We turned to his own letters; there were no more enclosures. Laboriously, word by word, the Alsatian translated, sometimes repeating a phrase. And then came one where she had no hesitation and saved me by a complete misunderstanding.

For centuries there has been little love lost between Austrians and Poles; there was a world of sarcasm in Carli's reference to *"unsere braven Polen,"* but Mme. Jacob did not know that. *"Nos braves Polonais,"* she proudly trumpeted. "Our valiant Poles. . . ."

"Hm," said the inspector, looking thoughtful. "Maybe we'll just send you back?"

I jumped up. "Shoot me first!"

In the ensuing pause the clock struck twelve, the sacred noon hour that nothing must disturb. The inspector rose to think my case over at lunch and then to investigate it further in Toulouse. My file went with him; I would remain under surveillance. Should a fingerprint check disclose other incriminating facts, I would, to start with, be sent to the women's prison in Toulouse.

The gendarmes followed the inspector; even gendarmes must have lunch. I was alone. Scattered all about were my possessions; only the little suitcase I had brought from Arcachon stood untouched in its corner, and when I opened it, I saw the swastikas on K.G.'s documents stare at me. I stuffed the papers into my blouse, ran across the corridor to the toilet, and tore the stuff to shreds before flushing it away. I did not faint until I was back in my room.

I was not allowed beyond the village limits, and twice a day, mornings and evenings, I had to report to the gendarmerie post. Secretly, from various towns in the vicinity, Gilbert mailed my letters to Paris. Answers were to go to his address, but he never received any; whether this was due to interference by Mme. Duval, the postmistress, we could not tell. Gilbert knew only that Irène Duval loathed letters in general and with reason; this was why she had become postmistress after her husband's sudden death forced her to go to work.

Gilbert remembered it all vividly; he had still been working on Jacques Duval's coffin when Irène begged him to come and look at something. It was a pack of letters from Jacques, written during his last business trip, on which he had had the accident. They were so moving Gilbert hardly dared to read them. Then Irène showed him the envelopes. They were addressed not to her but to Mélanie Gazette, the village seamstress. Her good friend Mélanie had not even waited for the funeral to send the dead man's love letters to Irène.

All through the funeral, at which Gilbert was a pallbearer, he could hear the widow sobbing. Afterwards, still in tears, she implored him to comfort her—and, of course, he never could bear to see a woman cry. Only his *petit frère* wouldn't play along that time with poor Irène. Accidents will happen, Gilbert said.

A real paradise, I thought, our Clairac. The sunflowers round the witches' cottages wilted. The beach restaurant was closed, the owner drafted. Dancing had ceased, with the young men away and the women alone with their intrigues.

Children skipped through the streets, for school was starting late this year due to the war. The children danced round and chanted, chiefly a ditty about the English who would fight to the last drop of French blood. Jeannot, however, preferred to run after Gilbert, who would lift the boy to his shoulders and carry him over to the shop like that—like a trophy. Underneath the sign of Dubois, *père et fils*, Jeannot liked to sit with me, or we played catch with his dog, Diane. *"Je t'aime—quand-même"*—it rang out of the shop between hammer blows.

Mornings and evenings Gilbert would escort me to the gendarmerie. No word regarding me came from Toulouse.

Probably they had forgotten all about me; there must be many more important cases, said Lefèbvre, who was getting used to us. "Don't waste your time," he said, chuckling, and seemed not displeased to find Gilbert had no one but me on his mind.

We did not waste our time. Not knowing how much we had, we used every minute and every place I could go, indoors or outdoors. The Roman temple was in my permitted area—it would have been restored that year, except for the war—and we would sit in the ruins or lie in their shelter, in the foliage that grew within, with only the moon watching. How long . . . ?

One day, unexpectedly, I did get word from Paris. Instead of a letter, Carli sent me a friend, his cousin Otto. Otto Frucht had stayed with us at the Hôtel de l'Univers. He told me what was happening to refugees in Paris. Carli and a few thousand others were isolated in the Stade Colombe, the sports arena that had become a detention camp. The *"ex-autrichiens"* among the inmates were pressured to volunteer for the Foreign Legion. Otto Frucht himself, a Czech-passport holder like Passer, was due to follow Passer into the Czech Army, though not as a volunteer.

Later, after the French collapse, Otto's unit was disbanded too late for him to get out of France; Clairac was the only possible haven he could think of. Gilbert put him up, and Otto managed to work for months in the carpenter's shop. When this got too dangerous, Gilbert's friend Martin gave him a job at the power plant outside the village; then Noguès, of our barbecue, hid him on his farm in the wilderness; and on the night when the gendarmes came from Bordeaux and Toulouse to round up all refugees, Gilbert and his anarchist friend Noguès drove Otto in a truck into the wilderness, *le maquis*, to other members of their resistance group. Eventually he made his way to Toulouse, where he remained. Driving from Toulouse with Otto and his French wife,

Maguy, I revisited Clairac in the spring of 1969 and heard his story.

It was on September 27, 1939, soon after Otto's arrival in Clairac, that Warsaw fell. For nineteen days the city held out desperately against overwhelming numbers and equipment, under bombardment and raids by dive-bombers, and to the end we heard the signal of Radio Warsaw, the three bars from Chopin's *Polonaise in A Major*. On the twenty-seventh, having shown themselves brave in every sense of the word, the Poles fell silent, and two days later Hitler and Stalin split the loot.

"All quiet in Clairac," I wrote to Carli at the camp in one of several letters that never reached him. "People talk about a *drôle de guerre*." In English they called it phony war, in German *Sitzkrieg*, in French *la drôle de guerre*. With their menfolk safely ensconced in the Maginot Line, the women of Clairac ran the village. At the hairdresser's, at the garage, even at the power plant, they took over; only at the carpenter's shop was there no change. I watched Gilbert cut boards and nail them together, mix paint and put it on, and I wanted to help, but he said this work was not learned in a hurry.

One morning there were knocks on my door again. My first thought was of the gendarmes, but then a woman's voice called, asking if M. Dubois was there. It turned out that his mother, though she never admitted knowing about us, had sent a neighbor who urgently needed a coffin; her husband had died in the night.

This time Gilbert let me help. He cut and painted the lid first, and when it dried before he had finished the rest of the coffin, he gave me a crucifix and a hammer to nail it on with. It was simple, he said. "Just hit hard."

In my eagerness I hit so hard that the Saviour's figure broke in two. I was aghast, but Gilbert glued the pieces together so skillfully that no one spotted the break, and despite my beginner's misfortune I was allowed to nail the Crucified on every coffin lid thereafter. Hitting Him more gently was easy, Gilbert said; the tough part was to get to hit Him at all. And when Mother Dubois came to the shop one day and found me doing this work, she looked on in amazement. "*L'autrichienne* is no worse than anyone else," she said afterward.

I was allowed to help with the grape harvest too, wearing the same wooden slippers and apron as the other women and carrying the same large basket to drop the grapes in. They were dark and sweet; it promised to be a good year. Where would I be when they drank this wine? The question ran through my mind as I stood picking grapes, gazing on the slopes, so like the Vienna Woods, along the Lot, on the bridge and the carpenter's shop and the witches' cottages— if only I could hold it fast, I thought, all of it. And I told Gilbert that someday I would write a novel about Clairac.

"A novel?" He shook his head. "You must write it as it is."

I couldn't, then; it was all much too close. I changed things, even names: Clairac turned into "St. C." and Gilbert into "Jean," and little Jeannot became "Pierrot." For a title I decided on *Dossier d'Amour*.

My official dossier remained in Toulouse, I suppose; the other accompanied me later, in the rucksack I carried all the way through France, and it lies on my desk now, in black and a slightly yellowed white. Reality stands in between. "You must write it as it is," Gilbert told me. Have I done so now? I hope so.

Gilbert liked to read stories set in his own part of the country, like those of Jean Giono, the Gascon writer. When he saw Pierhal's French translation of Horvath's *Youth without God* in my room one day and asked to borrow it, I was afraid the real meaning might escape him. He brought it back and said he loved it, though, one part in particular.

"Which?" I asked.

He surprised me ."The talk with the priest," he said. "When

he tells the teacher that God is the most terrible thing in the world." This from anticlerical Gilbert.

On November 15 the old church bell of Clairac rang for a wedding. I remember the date even though it was not of historic importance—in fact, the curé had hoped to consecrate a new bell on this occasion, but that plan too fell victim to the war. On the other hand, it was the war that caused the wedding. Mme. Lacoste, after so many years of hesitation, had suddenly resolved to marry Monsieur after all—for nothing else, it seemed, allowed their son to become legal co-proprietor of the hotel and therefore draft-exempt.

The wedding preparations galvanized all of Clairac. Even Gilbert, who never set foot in the church except to help carry in his coffins, felt that this festivity must not be missed. I got Mme. Gazette to modernize one of my two dresses, and at the fitting she told me that the wedding would effect a change in her own life: She would make friends again with Irène Duval, the postmistress, since both of them were going to be maids of honor. The groom wore an old tailcoat, made for the christening of his son and gaping rather wide in front now; a tall flower arrangement swayed on the unveiled head of the bride. Before her, in pink and sky-blue, walked her reconciled attendants.

A few sun rays fell through the stained-glass windows into the twilight of the church, heavy with incense. Tapers burned on the altar; before it the priest joined the hands of the two innkeepers and said, as always, "Until death do you part." Then *patron* and *patronne* exchanged rings and kisses, and behind a side altar, hidden so that no one saw us, Gilbert kissed me. "Now we are married," he said.

The wedding menu featured roast goose, but we were not invited. When the priest and the congregation followed the newlyweds to the Hôtel Les Glycines, we went back to the shop, bolted the door, drew the shades, and lay in the fragrant sawdust. Here too, inquisitive sun rays pierced the shades. By the well outside, Jeannot was playing with the vil-

116

lage children. "We must have a child, you and I," Gilbert said between kisses.

The dust grains danced in the air in bluish whirls. "A little Jeannot," I said softly. If we had a child, our happiness would survive us; we both felt that when we were one. . . .

From that day on we talked about our Jeannot. He had to study at the Sorbonne, I thought. But he had to learn a trade first, Gilbert decided.

As he found out about our secret, the chief of gendarmes, grinning broadly, gave me a permit to travel to Agen, the county seat of Lot-et-Garonne. Gaston's wife, who ran the garage in his absence, lent us a car for the trip, for two hundred francs. In France, where the birthrate was dwindling, French-born babies were wanted. Maybe for that reason Gilbert might get a marriage license after all—even for me.

They kept us waiting at the Prefecture—military personnel came first—but when our turn finally arrived, it didn't take a minute for them to say no. I ought to have known that under no circumstances could a Frenchman marry a woman without a *carte d'identité*.

"You'll get one after the war," Gilbert said confidently. "It isn't going to take very long. I want no one but you."

What did not take long, after we got back from Agen, was the arrival of my safe conduct to Paris. "This means that now you have to leave Clairac," the chief of gendarmes said, handing me the piece of paper. He sounded almost sorry. He had become used to me in the last half year.

"*Je t'aime*," Gilbert said on the bridge, kissing me for the last time. "*Tu reviendras*. You'll come back."

When I did come back, thirty years later, I first stopped a moment, alone, on the bridge in the spot where it curves down to the carpenter's shop. I wished I could take that moment with me. In fact, the view is now for sale on postcards, as are the views of the "unique beach" and of the one witches' cottage left standing.

The cottage is now a museum. Rickety wooden stairs lead

to a room in which Clairac's history hangs on the walls—
pictures that bring the centuries down to us. A young man,
Claude Martin, is curator of the collection. He recognized
Otto as soon as we came in, although Claude had been a
small boy at the time his father sheltered Otto. The museum is
Claude's hobby; he too makes his living at the power plant.
His father, long retired, rarely left the house nowadays,
Claude told Otto.

"Do you remember Gilbert Dubois?" I asked just before
leaving, when we bought the picture postcards.

"Of course," Claude said. "*Il était le coq du village.*" The
village cock. . . . I did not answer. Of Gilbert's death Otto
had written me over ten years ago, after a visit of his to
Clairac.

Claude advised against a call on the widow. She had re-
married, he said, and like many others she disliked talking of
old times. Just the same, while he took Otto and Maguy to
see his father, I quickly walked down to the bridge, past
the shop with the "NE PAS S'ARRÊTER" sign, and knocked on
the door of the house one can now plainly see on the postcard.

"*Qui est là?*" came from within. "Who is it?"

And I answered distinctly: "Madame Pauli, from America."

The door was opened, and two slanting cat's eyes looked
at me, astonished. "Come in," Madame said.

I complied. On the living room table a loaf of white bread
lay beside a glass of wine. "Excuse me," Madame said. "I've
only just come home to eat."

I stopped, embarrassed. "Please don't let me disturb you,
Madame."

She led the way to the window niche. "You're not disturb-
ing me," she said and offered me a seat. "I know your name.
It was so long after the war that you wrote. Gilbert showed
me your letter. He answered at once."

I remembered. "*Je t'embrasse,*" the letter closed, and the
lines before dealt with his children. "Jeannot must be quite
grown up by now," I said.

"Yes, Jean-Pierre is a student in Toulouse," Madame replied. "I call him Pierrot. Our daughter Nicole lives in Paris, with a painter. Oh, well, these children. . . ."

We looked at each other. The sun was setting over the hills outside, and a ray fell on her short hair. Like mine, it had a reddish glint. "It's a pity Gilbert isn't here to see you again," she said. "He would have enjoyed it so."

She was younger than I. "He might have been disappointed," I said.

She shook her head. "I don't think so. He talked about you so often. You're a writer—married, you wrote—do you have children?"

"No."

She asked no more questions. Without a break she talked on into the dusk. Her name was Juliette; Gilbert and she had been neighbors' children. Her first husband had been killed in the war. Her present husband, also widowed, had been one of Gilbert's companions; for nights on end they had been making the rounds together. But now, since her marriage, her husband would not speak of Gilbert anymore.

"It's been so long ago." She thought a moment. "What a gift for love he had, *n'est-ce pas?* It would have been wasted if he hadn't made so many happy."

Once, when he had sneaked out of her window again in the dead of night, she had followed him and had seen him take along a rifle. He was going out with the Maquis to free some prisoners. She did not know whether they succeeded. Another time she herself had to hide him during a search. She ran away from him several times, when she couldn't stand it any longer—all those other women—but she always came right back.

She talked and talked. *"Quel beau garçon. . . ."*

At the end, when his health deteriorated suddenly, he would let no one see him, no one but her. It was a brain tumor. Not till after the operation were they married. Then Gilbert wanted a church wedding and invited his sister and wept all through the ceremony—yes, with tears running down his face.

He never complained. He was cheerful to the end. He worked in the shop as long as he was able; it was closed only after he died. The house was hers now, and the children's. Some rooms she rented. Right now she had no vacancy.

"Another time, perhaps, when I come back," I said and got up. There were shadows creeping in the window.

"In another thirty years?" Madame asked on the way to the door.

"It'll be too late then," I replied on the threshold. "Or we'd have to meet somewhere else."

The slanting eyes narrowed in the twilight. "That's something Gilbert didn't believe in," Juliette said and held out her hand with a vague "*Au revoir.*" She stood in the door, slender in a gray suit, and the cat's eyes followed me to the village well across the street, where the women did their washing as of yore.

CHAPTER 7

In the Name
of Us All

The City of Light lay in darkness when I returned from Clairac late in November. The blinker light next to the Hôtel de l'Univers was twinkling blue, not red, due to the blackout regulations. Mme. Boucher had several vacancies and put me into another room facing the courtyard. "Forsaken smirk on pale impasse—that's Montparnasse, a mental quirk," wrote Walter Mehring.

We were reunited in our little hotel. The French PEN Club's intercession had induced the authorities to order Walter released from a detention camp, allowing him to go on rhyming.

K.G., never detained, had hired a Roumanian named Alex in Carli's place. He deplored Carli's stubborn refusal to volunteer for the Foreign Legion, like so many others. It was the one way to get out; now Carli was stuck and would soon be transferred to another camp, according to K.G.

I went back to work for him—having received a new

permis de séjour that would expire in less time than my old one and did not allow me to leave Paris—but it was not one of my fertile periods. Hardly any ideas occurred to me that would have been worth smuggling into the Third Reich. Manga Bell and I kept rummaging through whatever German telephone books were left at Parisian post offices, but most of the addresses we came back with turned out to be obsolete.

The table near the Luxembourg where we had sat stood empty, forsaken like the park in the November mists. Our circle had shrunk. Two new literary friends came to the hotel now and then to spend the long evenings with Mehring and me: Ernst Weiss and Hans Natonek. Although both wrote in the German language, they were Czech citizens past military age—which was why they had been left at liberty. The four of us would talk about the situation, not knowing where to turn. War had hardly lessened the esteem in which French Rightists held the German Führer; no one doubted that Pierre Laval, for example, was in touch with Hitler behind the government's back. What would become of us?

Weiss saw no hope. He was too tired and too sick, he said, to keep running. A stomach ulcer added to his depression, and as a medical doctor he knew he would not get rid of it. He had been at work on a novel, but no more—it was no use. "You do not live," he told me once. "You just write. What good is that for a woman?"

I was writing my *Dossier d'Amour*.

Sometimes K.G. would stray into the hotel, exuding confidence. The Maginot Line was a solid bulwark, he assured us; every time a German breakthrough had been whispered about, it had proved to be a canard. But one canard, which Wollenberg told us on November 30, proved a fact: The Russians had broken into Finland. "If we don't intervene now, we're lost," said Wollenberg. By "we" he meant the Western powers, and so did K.G., who was in hot disagreement: For "us" to wage a two-front war would be *la fin du tout.*

122

The wail of sirens rent the nights occasionally and left us wondering whether it was a test or the real thing. *"Les avions! Les avions!"* M. Boucher would shout, knocking on doors; everyone would scurry down to the nerve-rackingly narrow basement, and each time I wondered what would happen if the building above were hit and we were trapped under the rubble. I could feel myself suffocate. Some guests carried gas masks, but I didn't have one. K.G., as usual, heard only what he wished to hear. After each nocturnal alert he would announce that he had slept peacefully through it.

Nothing happened in Paris, really, in those early December days. In the camps there were no shelters; the imprisoned refugees were spared the choice of hiding or staying put. Carli was able to get a note to us during his transfer to a camp near Le Mans. He still balked at the Foreign Legion—because, he hinted, it was full of Nazi noncoms. Which nobody could deny.

Refugees were deemed unfit for regular army service that might pit them against their own ex-compatriots; on the other hand the French could not let them sit in the cafés of Paris either, rubbing elbows with *poilus* on furlough. This would have been an insult to the combat soldiers, even though there was no combat yet. (Later, far away, these rules became less rigid. In America refugees were promptly sworn in as soldiers and, before going overseas, as citizens; Carli, for instance, returned to France on D Day + 1 to interrogate Wehrmacht prisoners.)

The American colony in the *quartier* had shrunk as fast as our round table at the Tournon. The students and the artists had gone home; almost the only ones left were the newsmen. Eric Sevareid and his colleagues made frequent trips to the front, but as yet no foreign observer had seen the detention camps. Eric collected some articles that had appeared in America to the effect that the so-called assembly centers were no better than Nazi concentration camps, and he took them to the Ministry of Information. The idea of such reports circulating abroad distressed the propaganda people sufficiently to win an exception from the Ministry of the Interior: Eric, all by himself, was given a tour of the camps near Le Mans. He told me about it when he came back to Paris.

A wave of icy air had hit him when the commander of the first camp, a major of the French colonial army, personally led the way into one of the barracks. "Attention!" barked the major, and a line of shivering men—some in their teens, others in their sixties—scrambled to their feet, clutching blankets round their shoulders. Embarrassed, Eric, in his warm coat, passed down the line beside the camp commander and was glad when the review was over. The barrack building was more than a hundred feet long, and the one small iron stove in the center was cold. When they were out in the yard again and Eric pointed to a woodpile ringed by barbed wire, the major growled. "They're thieves, the *boche* bastards, every one of them. They were stealing the wood at night."

Eric thought he was mentally prepared for the next camp. He was wrong. His escort, a lieutenant, ushered him across the muddy grounds behind the barbed-wire fence, amid assurances that things had improved vastly. The inmates, obliged at first to sleep right in the mud, now had pallets of chicken wire; they had a latrine too where once there had been no toilet facilities whatever. "You should have seen it before," said the lieutenant. "There was nothing. Just a swamp."

A man in dirty rags came up, seeking to catch Eric's eye. "Please, sir," he stammered, "you know me." He was an Austrian, formerly Vienna correspondent for an Amsterdam daily. He pressed a slip of paper with his name and a Paris address into Eric's hand, tried to add something, choked on a sob, and was gone, engulfed in the crowd that suddenly surrounded Eric. Hundreds of filthy bearded figures seemed

124

to have sprung from nowhere, trying to make themselves heard in French, English, or German. Some were weeping. All looked like hoboes: a tenor from the Vienna Opera, a poet, a movie director, surgeons, lawyers, journalists, students. They pushed and shoved to get to the American, tugged at his sleeves, and scribbled notes to stuff into his pockets.

Eric stood there, helpless and feeling guilty. Somebody called his name. He turned. There was Carli, whom he almost failed to recognize. A scraggly Christ-like beard on sunken cheeks made Carli's eyes look larger, dark, and deep. Eric shuddered to see him like this; his throat tightened so he could hardly speak, and he looked away because there were tears in his eyes. They walked together to the wire gate, Eric holding a handkerchief to his face. They could not talk to each other; they found only a few stock phrases.

At the gate Eric took off his topcoat and gave it to Carli. Outside a car with some French officers was waiting for him. Inside the gate, a few steps from the car, Carli slipped one arm around Eric's shoulder, and Eric turned away from him and began to cry.

The scene remained unforgotten. It went into the book Eric Sevareid called *Not So Wild a Dream*.

The year 1939 was drawing to a close. Christmas approached on the calendar. In the Rue de la Paix the shop windows glistened with jewels, as they always did, and Charvet featured silk scarves in the French national colors of blue, white, and red. At the Casino de Paris Maurice Chevalier sang for soldiers and civilians: *"Paris sera toujours Paris. . . ."*

Along the Rhine and in the Maginot the soldiers shivered in their bunkers. It was a cold winter. Carli had been in camp more than three months. Sevareid reported on the camps but could do nothing to help; the only change was in his own situation.

Some months earlier a phone call for him had come from

the London bureau of the Columbia Broadcasting System. Edward R. Murrow, the bureau chief whom Eric had briefly met once, was calling: Would Eric try broadcasting radio reports to New York? "I don't know much about your experience," Ed Murrow said in his familiar voice, but added that he liked young Sevareid's ideas and style. He wanted facts, not sensations; if there was no news, Eric should just say so—"I have an idea people might like that." A trial broadcast would be set up for the New York office. "Maybe something will come of it," Murrow concluded.

What came of it was Eric Sevareid's career. He spent Christmas Eve broadcasting from a fort of the Maginot Line, where the soldiers had turned the munitions room into a kind of chapel. The Midnight Mass was celebrated, carols rang out, and the message of peace on earth faded away in the night.

Next morning Eric found another Christmas story. He heard it from the *poilus* guarding the French end of the Strasbourg-Kehl bridge. On the night of the twenty-fourth the Germans had set up a Christmas tree atop their pillbox on the far side of the bridge. They had even lit candles on it to show how unworried they were about the French guns and gunners. The sight rankled, and around midnight a French private took off his boots and crept across the bridge, alone and unarmed, and brought back the German Christmas tree. Eric was shown the trophy with the burned-down lights.

I spent Christmas Eve with Lois and the Sevareids' few friends who had remained in Paris. Ted Meltzer was no longer with us. Encouraged by Eric's success, he too had applied for a job as a radio correspondent. Murrow and William Shirer had confirmed that more reporters were wanted for the American networks. Ted waited until just before the holidays; then he suddenly lost patience. "Don't leave me alone on Christmas," he had heard from Charlotte in Minnesota. He was on the high seas when the cable from

New York arrived at our hotel with a broadcasting-job offer for him. All that we could do was forward it to Minnesota. Too late—Ted had missed his chance.

A second case of homesickness thinned our ranks when Vera Liessem failed to rejoin us. The letters from her Spanish tour had sounded more and more desperate: Her nightclub acts were successful enough, but certain other activities, not spelled out in the contract, were also expected of her, and her refusals led to canceled bookings. Her money ran out. From us she got only bad news; from Hamburg her mother wrote sadly about loneliness. One day Vera had enough. After all, the Horvaths had also gone back to Germany. "Please don't be mad at me," her letter ended.

"We get to be fewer and fewer," Odon had said, ages ago.

It was a quiet Christmas Eve. Only Lois had a surprise for us: She was expecting a baby. Hopefully, all would go well. Most French doctors were at the front by then, but she had found an aged obstetrician who worked at a military hospital in Paris and came to see her on his days off. He found everything in order and marveled only at how fast she was gaining weight.

I was not expecting "Jeannot" anymore. . . . It was better this way, in my situation. I was waiting for Gilbert. He had a hard time getting away now, with Dubois *père et fils* swamped with orders for the army. This brought in money, at least; but over the holidays, Gilbert wrote, he was going to lock up and come to me.

He really came to Paris, and we did see each other again. He looked different in his gray Sunday suit and wore a tie with his silk shirt. It was a Christmas gift from his sister Janine, who liked modern things only. Both of us thought of the cradle. "How nice Jeannot would have looked in it," said Gilbert. Then he kissed the tears off my cheeks: "We'll just have to wait till the war is over."

127

My girl friends followed us with envious eyes. They all fell for him, of course, and took him for an architect because he talked mostly of Clairac and its old houses. We did not disillusion them. We wanted to be alone; we were inseparable day and night, enjoying the few hours left.

One night we were disturbed by the usual sirens and M. Boucher shouting, *"Les avions! Les avions!"*

Gilbert held me tight. "Wouldn't it be sweet to die together like this?"

I stopped being afraid. We stayed where we were.

"Chérie," he asked when we had to say good-bye, "will you think of me every night, the way I'll be thinking of you?" He kissed me. "I'm not up to mischief anymore. *Je t'aime."*

I never went to the basement shelter again.

The New Year's mood in Paris was tinged with panic. The French were afraid of defeat and afraid of winning. They remembered their last victory over the Germans; it had not done them much good. They were ready to fight for their country if they must, but not to take the fight to the enemy. They would let fugitives from Hitler live in their midst, but they would not leave them at large, and they would certainly not arm them against Hitler. On a Parisian railway platform, about to board a train for one of his trips to the front, Eric Sevareid ran into Carli again; under the topcoat Eric had left him in camp Carli wore a uniform several sizes too large. He had become a *prestataire,* a member of the "unarmed military labor force" in which detained refugees were now used to build fortifications.

Carli had a three-day pass, and we were happy to have him back among us even if it could not last. We wondered when we would meet again, how we would ever find each other again if the tides of war swept us apart. Carli had an idea. "Clairac," he said—this was where we should write, where we should try to go if we lost contact. And we laughed, thinking of a joke that had made the rounds of the Vienna coffeehouses during World War I: "See you after the war at six."

While Carli was heading south—why fortifications were being built there remained a mystery—Rolf Passer in a Czech lieutenant's uniform came through on his way north to the front. "We're going to be thrown into the forward lines, to cover the French," said Passer, ready for anything. His was an unfamiliar uniform in Paris, and when we walked down the boulevard together, we drew curious glances. It amused him, and he told me of a funny letter he had written to me, to Clairac, about the numbers of horses and men under his command. "It almost got me court-martialed," he said, grinning.

"Me, too," I said. The war wasn't so funny after all. He and I also agreed to keep in touch via Clairac, if necessary.

Paris was awash with rumors. There was talk of pending deals and impending offensives, of troop buildups, even of embarkations. French units were said to be bound for Finland to fight Russians, not Germans. Eric Sevareid found a hint at such a plan in the semiofficial *Le Temps*. He decided to report it. His forecast of intervention in Finland echoed all over America. It also produced a sharp Russian warning and, back in France, an official statement that the enterprise—by then abandoned—had been intended only to protect the Swedish iron mines from the Germans. Despite the lame excuse, the shock of learning that France had been on the brink of war with Russia too cost Premier Daladier his job; it went to Paul Reynaud, a moderate man who later on assured himself of a footnote in history by begging for "clouds" of American planes, right away. The Ides of March brought a Russo-Finnish armistice.

Ex-General Wollenberg disappeared—to a camp in the south, we learned later. A good many colleagues met at this camp for the "politically suspect": the journalist Leo Lania, on account of his Russian birth; the novelist Leonhard Frank, on account of his Leftist leanings. Other inmates, like

the Austrian Paul Friedländer and the German Willi Münzenberg, were Communists who had denounced Stalin's pact
with Hitler.

The four of us, Mehring, Weiss, Natonek, and I, still met
behind the drawn shades of my room at the Hôtel de
l'Univers, talking in whispers. Women too were being
rounded up in the streets now. Two *flics* stopped me at the
corner of the boulevard, demanded my *carte d'identité*, and
took me to the Prefecture when they found I did not have
one. I produced my valid *permis de séjour* to no avail.
"We're getting you out of Paris for your own good," said
the *commissaire*. "In the women's camp at Gurs you'll be
quite safe."

I stood there, flanked by the two who had brought me in.
"May I go get my things?" I asked quietly, boiling inside.

The answer was no; I had to go right away. I looked at this
French police official as I had at the S.S. man on the train to
Switzerland. "How many women are in that camp?" I
inquired.

A few thousand.

"And how many guards?"

He shrugged. He did not know.

"*Ah, ça,*" I said, hissing through my teeth. "Go ahead; just
send me down there. You'll see."

The official frowned and hesitated a moment before slam-
ming his fist on the desk. "*Nous ne voulons pas de vous,*" he
snarled, as if consigning me to perdition.

We don't want any part of you. . . . I didn't stop to see what
the other *flics* were doing. I was out the door, in the hallway,
in the street, running like a hunted beast. Ashen-faced and
out of breath, I arrived at the hotel and found Mehring
talking excitedly into the telephone. At the sight of me he
hung up.

When I failed to return, he had called Comert once again
and begged him to intercede, only to be told that the minister
plenipotentiary could do nothing: The government had

decreed that all female refugees be moved south, to Gurs in the Pyrenees, for safety.

"Protective custody," I sneered, and from then on I detoured around police uniforms like an escaped convict. I did not dare set foot in the Prefecture even when my *permis de séjour* expired. Before long, we would all expire anyway.

Through Mme. Clairouin, a Parisian literary agent with whom Carli and I had been dealing, I received a curious job offer: Would I go to Algiers to teach German to a colonial official's family and to transmit certain messages on occasion? I understood: An espionage network was being set up in case France fell. It was my chance to get out of Paris, out of the trap, out of danger, but I could not bring myself to take it. I belonged with my friends. Mousy little Denise Clairouin later became a heroine of the Resistance, was caught in the end, and died under Gestapo torture.

One day, visiting Lois Sevareid again, I found her pale and distraught. X-rays at the hospital had produced a new surprise: She was expecting twins. The birth, due in April, might be difficult; besides, there was a risk of losing the children between now and then. Lois spent the next three months flat on her back, hardly daring to move.

Eric saw his wife and the world simultaneously heading for a crisis. On April 9 the Germans launched a blitzkrieg against Denmark and Norway. There was no stopping them. A fleet of Danish fishing boats took refugees across the sound by night to neutral Sweden; Annemarie Selinko's Danish husband went to Sweden with her and on to England, later, as ambassador. The Swedish ore got into the headlines again when an Anglo-French expedition landed in the frozen north of Norway, at Narvik—too late.

We saw troops marching through Paris, but we were not allowed to leave the city. There were nooses around our necks, and we could feel them tighten as the stories came to us firsthand from Eric Sevareid. On April 25 he had to ask a colleague to broadcast for him while he got Lois to a hospital he had chosen in the suburb of Neuilly and paced outside the maternity ward all day and through the night. Once the doctor came out of the delivery room, looked at Eric, and went back in without a word. Then he reappeared, hands all bloody, and lit a cigarette with a tired nod to the husband. "I think it will go," he said. "For a time I wasn't so sure."

Minutes later a nurse rushed out, yelling, "*Deux beaux garçons!*" It was the first piece of good news Eric had been able to bring us in a long time. When I got out to Neuilly and to Lois's room at the Clinique St. Pierre, she was lying with the children in her arms, quietly happy. Eric had left for French North Africa to prepare broadcasting facilities in the event of an attack by Hitler's Italian ally, who was expected to join the war any moment.

On the night of May 9 M. Boucher did not shout "*Les avions*" as usual when the sirens wailed. "*Les bombes, les bombes!*" he screamed for the first time.

Planes thundered over the rooftops. I stayed in bed, thinking of Gilbert—but dying like that would not have been sweet at all. In the morning we heard that Paris had not been hit but that the Germans had invaded three countries at once: Luxembourg, Belgium, and Holland, which was said to be putting up desperate resistance. There were many victims in Rotterdam and elsewhere. Horvath's publisher leaped to his death from a window, as Friedell had in Vienna —but this time there was no misunderstanding.

Radio Paris broadcast the calls for the reserves. Hordes of officers and men flocked to the terminals and into waiting troop trains. No trains were waiting for us, but streams of new and different refugees started pouring down from the north—Belgians and Dutch, their countries overrun. In London Neville Chamberlain, the man of "peace in our time," made way for Winston Churchill, who formed a national government and recruited a home guard of civilians armed with sporting guns and butcher knives.

Eric never got to North Africa. Soon he was back in Paris, racing in a taxi to the hospital in Neuilly. He arrived at midnight, just as the staff was evacuating women and babies. They had forgotten Lois. He found her alone in a dark room, wide eyes fixed on the door behind which she had been left lying helplessly for hours. Some thousand-franc notes finally procured a nurse and an ambulance that looked like a hearse but served to get Lois and the twins to a small inn outside Paris, where they would be safe till Eric could find passage for them to America. It was only for the children's sake that Lois agreed to leave at all.

The only American ship due to sail, the *Manhattan* out of Genoa, was booked solid. Eric paid for reservations on the Italian liner *Rex* and left for the army press headquarters at Cambrai. Discovering that this was no place to hear the truth about the fighting, he and another American returned to Paris. The trip was endless, punctuated by the sound of planes and bombs in the night. At one long halt in open country they suddenly saw flashes on the horizon and heard the faint rumble of artillery. Counting seconds, calculating distance and direction, they placed the firing well inside the French lines—"There could be no doubt," Eric wrote later; "the Germans had broken through."

In Paris white-clad women ran along the crowded platforms with pails of milk, shouting, "Only for the children, please—only for the children!" Eric found a phone. The United States Embassy confirmed the breach in the line, and so did well-informed French friends, but as yet no one outside France had an inkling. No hint got past the censors. Eric cabled one line; like our "Uncle Emil" during the Anschluss, it looked innocuous but tallied with a code Eric had given a colleague to take to New York months before. The cable went through and scooped the world.

At his apartment Eric heard from the Italian Line that the *Rex* would not sail. Why not? "Orders from the Duce." Obviously he was set to take the plunge. A personal plea to the manager of the United States Lines yielded a cabin on the *Manhattan* for Lois and the babies. Seeing them off at the Gare de Lyon, Eric had a shock: His wife and the two baskets she carried, with a twin in each, had suddenly disappeared! Then a cluster of cooing, clucking French-women broke up, and the central attraction turned out to be his wife and her brood. . . . Lois and the babies reached New York on June 11, the day Eric had to flee from Paris.

Paris, in that first week of June, was a sluice with wave upon wave of fugitives pounding through it. The Belgian Army had surrendered and was on its way to German prison camps, but the rest of the Belgians, women, children, old men, seemed to have packed up and joined the people of invaded northern France in a rush to Paris. They came from the north and left toward the south, with the floodgates open for all except us. We were watched for, turned back, put under arrest at every exit.

June 4 brought the first serious bombing raid. The Air Ministry and the Citroën plant were hit, and I saw smoke clouds billow over the city and roll down the Champs-Élysées. That same evening we heard Winston Churchill on the radio. The British had just given up Dunkirk, their last toehold on the continent, but their new leader did not sound like Chamberlain. "We shall go on to the end," he said. "We shall fight on the beaches, we shall fight on the landing grounds. . . . We shall never surrender."

Where we were there was no sign of such a spirit, no glimpse of hope. Where should we turn, with Europe crumbling around us? America—nowhere but in America might there be a haven. "But who will get us over there?" asked Ernst Weiss in my blacked-out hotel room.

Hans Natonek had an idea. Thomas Mann was in America; if we wrote to him, he might persuade people to help us over.

"Natonek, you're the true poet among us." Mehring laughed sarcastically.

Natonek did not stop fantasizing. "A telegram," he said, "we must send Mann a telegram. We've got to get out of here—they must help us get out. . . . "

I was beginning to listen.

"The four of us, of all people," Mehring said, jeering. Then he suddenly turned to me: "I could, perhaps. . . . I know Mann pretty well."

A moment of silence; then Weiss spoke again. "Yes, leave me out. It's no use anyway."

I looked at him, at his hollow cheeks. "All or none," I said.

We were too few, said Weiss. Or too many, said Mehring. I do not remember who finally thought of it; we just sat batting ideas around until the right expression came up: "in the name of us all." That was what we would cable and sign, we four in the name of all the rest—of all those mired here in France, including Thomas Mann's own brother Heinrich, who was in a camp somewhere, Lion Feuchtwanger, Franz Werfel, Leonhard Frank, the playwright Walter Hasenclever, and whoever else was still living. In the name of us all.

We sent the cable to Thomas Mann in Princeton, New Jersey, on the ninth of June. It would probably never reach him and would accomplish nothing, said Weiss, but he signed. The common concern tied us more firmly together; the torn circle closed again. I felt grateful to be part of it, comforted, and inwardly at home.

"Wherever you may be, by the broiling Dead Sea or on a prairie farm, there's equal sorrow," it says in Mehring's "Emigrants' Song." We belonged together. If no answer came to our cry for help, at least we had asked. At least we had something to wait for.

On June 10 someone knocked on my door. At every knock we feared to be arrested; but when I opened, a pretty young woman stood outside. "Gilbert sent me," she said. And

I recognized Mara, the slim, dark one who had been at the barbecue on Noguès's farm.

"Where is Gilbert? " I asked.

"In Clairac," she answered. "We're driving there tonight. My car is waiting in front of the hotel. Your last chance—there are no more trains."

Tonight, I thought; Clairac, Gilbert—and then I saw Mehring beside me, as though forgotten. "Can I take my friend along?"

She shook her head. "I have two friends with me who must get out at once. There's room for only one more."

I could not leave by myself. "It's forbidden for foreigners to leave Paris anyway," I blurted out. "For you it's different, but I can't come—Gilbert will understand. Thanks a million times, and good luck to you."

"*Au revoir,*" Mara called from the stairs, not looking back.

Mehring, chalk-white, stood beside me. "I won't go without you," I told him. And as in Vienna once upon a time, he spent the night at the telephone, calling vainly for help.

In the morning he heard at the Quai d'Orsay that the government also had fled overnight to an undisclosed location—"moved in order to save Paris," as the radio put it later on that June 11. The capital had been declared an open city—open to the Germans. Mehring heard it and broke down.

I called K.G. He spoke of a new French defense line behind the Loire, which we had to get to, and told me to come over right away, with only the bare necessities. I took the necessities and Mehring, who packed nothing but his manuscripts. We had to cross the Luxembourg; the gardens lay as empty as the streets. Anyone who had not run away as yet seemed to be hiding.

K.G. was busy packing. He took a look at Walter and said, "I see. . . . I hope we'll have room." Alex, the new secretary, had gone for a car. Getting out of town would be no trick, according to K.G.—the highways weren't watched any longer—but there was no time to waste. German armor had supposedly been sighted from Montmartre, he said, as he jammed more stuff into flat suitcases.

It was high noon by the time Alex returned, with a Roumanian girl friend I did not know. K.G. seemed to have expected her. Her name was Lily, and she would come with us; the car was waiting downstairs. "And Walter?" I asked.

K.G. nodded. "He's so little, we'll get him in somehow." I left my suitcase behind, taking only the rucksack. Walter, clutching his manuscripts, squeezed in between us. Alex strapped K.G.'s flat suitcases to the roof of the car. We did not know what was in them. Then we moved off, with Alex at the wheel, across Boulevard Montparnasse and on to the Porte d'Orléans. It suddenly struck me that we had not said a word to Weiss and Natonek.

K.G. shrugged his shoulders. "What for? We can't help them."

Natonek made his way out with another group; eventually we found each other again. Ernst Weiss—or his body, rather —was found in Paris by the Germans. He had opened his veins, and first, to make quite sure, the ex-M.D. had taken poison. We had deserted him that day, and I've never forgiven myself.

The empty Boul' Mich lay behind us; those who remained in the Latin Quarter were looking for holes to crawl into. We passed Montparnasse Cemetery, and at the Porte d'Orléans we got stuck for the first time in an immense jam of autos inching their way out of town like a giant caterpillar. In the sky above we saw planes circle, but no bombs fell on the open city.

Soon we were stuck again. The gears ground under Alex's trembling hands. We would have made better time on foot, but K.G. declared that we must not leave the car; it must not fall into the hands of the Germans. And we? it ran through my mind.

Over the Route Nationale the planes circled low enough for us to see the markings on their wings. They swooped down, roaring past on what seemed like a level with the tree tops along the road, and we thought we could hear the hiss and rattle of machine-gun bursts in the air. Alex kept looking upward; we almost landed in a ditch. "Keep your eyes on the road," I said, grabbing for the wheel.

We changed places. I drove on, though I had neither a driver's license nor any other valid document. It made no difference any more; nobody bothered with us. We were just a part of the fugitive tide.

Time moved on, but we didn't. I kept shifting forward and back; we were stuck again and again. The caterpillar writhed on the spot, to no purpose. The gas gauge quivered around the zero mark. "If we just make the next village," K.G. said, "we'll fill her up."

The night passed, and by morning we had to push the little car. It was heavier than it looked. At last we reached a village, half of its population gone. There was no gasoline, but K.G. managed to buy a bicycle that would take him to Étampes, not much farther ahead; we were to wait in the car for him to bring back a few liters of fuel.

We waited. There was no more need to push. The whole stream of cars had ground to a halt and stood motionless, bumper to bumper. People on foot and in ox carts passed right and left. Night fell again, and what seemed like sheet lightning ripped the darkness to the south, followed by the roll of distant thunder.

At dawn a rumor swept along the endless traffic jam, passing mouth to mouth, from car to car: Paris had fallen— the *boches* had entered the city—they were coming. I said we couldn't just stay here. Waiting for K.G. was useless; he would never come back. But Alex and Lily both insisted that we had to wait, that we mustn't leave the car.

Mehring's lips were white. "You're Roumanians," he told the pair; "nothing will happen to you."

138

I had not even thought of that. Walter was the most endangered of us all; his name had been on Goebbels's first list. He was lost if the Nazis got hold of him. I took his hand. "You can't stay."

We got out and looked for our things. Alex gave me an angry look; Lily shrugged her shoulders. "If K.G. should come back," I said, "tell him we're sorry."

Alex threw my rucksack out of the car. "If you meet him," he said, "give him our regards. We're staying with the car."

In fact, we did not hear of K.G. again until long after the collapse. It had been impossible to turn back; the Roumanians had waited in vain. When the Germans caught up with them, they were brought back to Paris as "allies," suffered no harm, and escaped later. To keep the car from falling into German hands they had set fire to it at the last moment; due to the mass of papers in K.G.'s suitcases it had burned like a tinder-box. Not even Alex and Lily had known that hidden among the propaganda material had been thousands of British pound notes.

The car was soon out of sight as Walter and I went on alone on foot. I carried the rucksack; Walter's fingers gripped the little suitcase with his manuscripts. We left the main highway underneath the circling planes and walked southward into the graying dawn, never looking back.

CHAPTER 8

No Exit

At sunrise we reached Étampes. It was in ruins—hence the sheet lightning of the past night. Propped against a half-crumbled door, a woman stood petrified, staring in dumb terror at a sky that was now blue and empty. We approached her and asked for directions. She did not stir. Then we saw her wide-open eyes, as blue and empty as the sky.

We quickly passed the dead woman, trying not to step on other corpses that lay about the street. We almost ran through this ghost town and out again; by side roads, to avoid the German bombers, we hurried from village to village, through forests, across open fields. We did not know the way, only the direction: south. . . .

Suddenly there were gendarmes on our heels, but this time we were not the target. The butts of their rifles pounded on the farmhouse doors: "Get up, everyone! Pack! Take just what's necessary!" Stunned faces showed in doors and windows. No one understood what was the matter until the gendarmes explained the evacuation order: "The *boches* are coming from Paris."

Then the whole countryside came to life. The peasants piled onto carts whatever they could and threw bales of hay atop their other possessions so the horses and oxen could be fed en route. Men and women with small children on their backs trudged alongside the vehicles. Livestock was set loose lest it starve in the barns. Cattle roamed the fields aimlessly, heads high in the air as though sniffing imminent doom. They trampled the ripening grain and now and then lowed fearfully.

Amidst horse-drawn wagons and ox carts and men and women and crying children we walked southward, ever southward, in the mass migration. Dogs ran back and forth, barking. We were in the middle of a panorama: a people in flight, leaving house, farm, and fields behind them. The shops we passed were mostly closed; only at long intervals could we pick up even a loaf of bread. The evacuation order followed us with rifle butts: "The Germans are coming."

The exodus was later said to have been instigated by the Germans themselves to block the highways. In any case, the result was that no military transport could get through, and we did not do much better. For hours we were lying at the roadside.

In Walter the chaotic flight wrought a transformation. The eternal skeptic turned into an optimist. Danger seemed to lend inexhaustible energies to the elfin figure by my side.

"I've never gone in for sports, so I don't get tired," he said, mocking me, when I reached the point of collapse. I could not walk another step. My feet were bleeding. I sprawled in a ditch, with Walter kneeling beside me: "Look over there—there's smoke coming out of a chimney. Come on, please. Come, it's only a few steps."

"You go," I said. "Just leave me here. I'm through."

He tried to lift me, to find the argument that would be most persuasive: "In Orléans there will be coffee again," he said.

What a poet you are, I thought. "All I need is a bed," I told him, knowing full well that this too was impossible.

"Yes," he replied, "I'm going to find you a bed. Wait here; I'll be right back."

He ran off. I closed my eyes. He would never come back, no more than K.G. had. It did not matter. I was worn out. I wanted to sleep, only to sleep. . . .

Walter shook me awake. "Come to bed," he said, urging, and pulled me along to a farmhouse. The bed belonged to a soldier killed in the fighting; Walter had talked to the widow. His plaint—"My wife is lying half dead in a ditch over there"—had moved her heart.

The woman took us for Belgian refugees. She let me sleep in her dead husband's bed all night, and in the morning she gave us bread and coffee. And surprisingly, I was able to go on.

"In Orléans we can rest up," Walter said to comfort me. "From there on it will be easier—there may even be trains— and we'll get to America in the end. I'm sure of it—I promise."

His optimistic imagination almost made me laugh. Behind us the *boches* were advancing; above us their planes drew vapor circles in the sky to mark the spots on which to drop the next bomb load.

"*Nous sommes perdus*—we're lost!" screeched the people in the marked area, scurrying out of the circle of death. Their dispersion threw the mass flight into wild confusion; it became a jumble of despair as the bombs began to fall. We jumped into a ditch, hugged the ground, took cover like well-drilled recruits—instinctively, without command. Dive-bombers swooped down, engines roaring, machine guns spitting.

I shut my eyes. I did not want to see death, but I heard it come closer and closer. Through the din Walter yelled, "Over there!"

I looked up and saw a few soldiers under a big tree across the road, using the massive trunk as a shield against strafing. One of them stood upright, pressed to the tree, and waved to us. Walter started to crawl over; I drew him back into the ditch. Then a bomb hit the tree, and the soldier crumpled and did not get up again. Dear God, I thought, if one of us is to go, let it be me, not Walter—he wants so much to live. . . .

Another bomb burst near us. We stayed in the ditch till the infernal noise had ceased and the vapor circle in the sky was fading. It was not needed any more. The planes had done their work. All that remained in the shadow of the swastikas was a circular moonscape with dead people and animals.

Only one of the soldiers under the tree had survived. He came over to us. *"Passez le pont,"* he said, *"et vous serez tranquils."* Cross the bridge, and you'll have peace. *Peace. . . .*

We stumbled on toward the Loire, the river that was to be the new defense line.

When the fugitive tide swept us into Orléans on June 16, it was like entering a mammoth Étampes. The city was bombed out, deathly quiet; here and there men were still digging for bodies. Then the planes returned. Sirens wailed; wedged in a mass of people, we were pushed across a back yard and down into a cellar. Our eyes needed time to get accustomed to the dark. I heard strange murmurings from a corner; after awhile I could make out a group of bearded, caftan-clad men huddling in prayer. "Kaddish," Mehring whispered to me. "They're saying Kaddish. It's the Jewish prayer for the dead."

Outside, sirens wailed and bombs exploded. Each time one burst, a young mother next to me spread her arms and flung

144

herself over her child. The child screamed. So did Walter, at the next hit.

"Don't scare the child," I called to him. He shut up.

The mother looked at me. "They'll blow up the bridges this evening," she said.

She had the child in her arms. "What's his name?" I asked. A crash drowned out her answer; again she threw herself on top of her child.

The bridges—I realized suddenly what she meant. We had to get there, to get across. "Who will blow them up?" I tried to outshout the explosions. "The Germans or the French?"

No one heard me till the magic sound of "All clear" changed the prayers for the dead into a rush for the exit. It was full of debris; broken doorposts and pieces of roof tiles had to be cleared away before we could climb out. The back yard was strewn with shattered glass. Shoes were cut to ribbons; it no longer mattered. The air was heavy with smoke, but nothing was burning along the street where we were; we saw only the reflection of fires in the city, right and left. Everyone was in a hurry to get to the bridge ahead— men, women, children, vehicles large and small. Only the dead were left behind.

We brought up the rear of the procession until we came to a truck that was being filled with gasoline; there was still fuel in Orléans. The driver filled not just his tank but also a number of large cans. The cans were being loaded onto the truck, and people were climbing aboard with them; the seat by the driver's side was free, so I jumped up on it, and Mehring followed, squeezing in behind me as the truck began to move. We caught up with the end of the vehicle column and rolled on, slowly, toward the Loire. The cathedral clock —still running—showed ten minutes after eight when we came to a halt at the bridgehead.

High above, the planes were drawing their long loops. We crawled on slowly, very slowly. Halfway across the bridge we stopped again, with the river beneath and the planes circling above.

I saw the driver's hands shake on the wheel as Alex's had outside Paris. This time, I knew, I must not make a move. In the back of the truck men, women, and children crouched motionless between the gasoline cans. It would not take a bomb to blow us sky-high—a stray bullet would do it, a ricochet, anything hitting the truck. Then, out of the sky, a plane dived straight at us.

"*Il pique*," Mehring shrilled, got out from behind me, and jumped. It was quite a jump to the pavement, but he landed on his feet, took off, and kept on going—a dwarfish shadow flitting past the solid line of cars toward the south bank of the Loire.

Our driver stepped on the gas. There was a jolt, a screeching of brakes, another jolt: We had rammed the car ahead of us. The dive-bomber hung there slantwise in the air.

Was he banking to return for another run? If I jumped down after Walter, there was going to be a panic. The car ahead began to move. We followed suit, crawled a few steps, and were stuck again. The plane leveled off and flew away into the dusk.

It was dark by the time we reached the other bank. The driver halted. Not to rest—just to put me off his truck. "*Nous ne voulons pas de vous*," he snarled. We don't want any part of you. . . . Where had I heard this before?

The truck pulled away, uphill, and disappeared. The vehicles ahead of it were gone; the people who had crossed the bridge on foot were long gone. I looked around for the soldiers manning the "new defense line"—none were in sight. I stood alone on the south bank of the Loire.

Suddenly there was a blinding flash behind me, followed by thunder. I looked back: There was no bridge anymore, only debris still plunging into the river, and clouds of smoke veiling the sea of flames on the north bank, from which I had come—the flames of Orléans.

By their light I saw Walter. He was lying on the ground, outstretched, motionless—dead?

I ran to him. He clung to me. We were still alive.

The French themselves had destroyed the bridge to hinder the German advance, but they had waited till the tail end of the refugee parade was safely south of the Loire. We, of course, knew nothing about this as we desperately searched for cover; we saw only the giant birds of the Luftwaffe hovering in the red sky over Orléans.

We spent the night under shrubbery and started heading south again at the break of dawn, uphill, away from the river, where pieces of the bridge stuck up out of the water like broken limbs. Fog and drifting smoke hid a roadblock ahead until we stumbled right into it, until barbed wire ripped my skirt and caught at my legs, and when we looked around for help we saw the cannon. A semicircle of field guns, painstakingly camouflaged with green, stood in a clearing—open-mouthed, abandoned, their crews decamped. Where were they? Where were we?

La Loire, *la gloire*, la Loire. . . . My thoughts ran in circles, as we did. Just get away; keep going. . . . From clearing to clearing we stumbled, over roots and stumps and fallen trees; a logging trail finally led to a highway crossing. A sign said, "TOURS," above a number of kilometers. Along the road came ragged figures of fugitives like ourselves. Where were they going? To Tours, they said; there the Germans would certainly meet resistance. After all, the government was at Tours.

A few soldiers sat by the roadside; they had white handkerchiefs tied to their rifles and waved them at us. "What are you waiting for?" we called over.

"*La paix, seulement la paix*," they called back. Peace,

nothing but peace. They had rifles, they said, but no ammunition. *"Nous sommes sans défense, madame."*

We sat down with them, and I wrapped a fresh handkerchief around my bleeding feet. My shoes were shredded; I threw them away and found a pair of sandals in my rucksack, but we had nothing to eat, not a crust of bread. "I'm so hungry," I said, more to myself than to anyone. I was starving. No money could buy food anymore.

The soldier next to me dug into his pocket and came up with some chocolate. "Take it," he said. "We've had nothing else for days; I throw up when I smell it."

I shared the crumbled chocolate bar with Walter. It tasted bitter, but we swallowed it greedily. A canteen of water was passed around; we would have liked to offer the men something in return, but we had nothing. Mehring sat empty-handed—and now, all of a sudden, it struck him: His precious manuscripts were gone.

"C'est la fin du tout," he said. It was the end.

"La paix, seulement la paix," the soldiers cried, waving their rifles with the white handkerchiefs.

And like an answer the huge birds of prey reappeared above us: In V formations, open ends toward Orléans, points aimed at Tours, where they might still be resisted, they flew downriver over our heads to draw new vapor circles. Walter jumped up and ran, as on the bridge. I ran after him. We scurried across the fields like stampeding cattle, without knowing where, aimlessly, senselessly, trampling the grain as fast as our legs would carry us.

A terrible noise stopped us in our tracks. It did not come from the sky, but it made the earth tremble. A monster crawled behind a clump of trees; not until it came into full view were we certain that it was nothing more than a tractor plow. An old man sat between the giant wheels, and we waved and ran up to him, pleading for a ride.

The noise lessened slightly. The tractor stopped. Walter

climbed to the edge of the driver's seat, and I somehow got on behind him, holding onto the draw bar when we moved off. The din was earsplitting. Walter kept slumping forward, and I kept shouting, "Look out! You'll fall off," but I could not hear my own voice. I found a scrap of paper and a pencil in my pocket; it was hard work writing on my lap on the shaking, jolting monster, but I managed to scrawl, "DON'T FALL ASLEEP," in large letters. The next time Walter's head drooped, I pinched him and held the paper under his nose. He read, and for the rest of the way he sat bolt upright.

The ride ended at a village inn. The old man went in, and we followed, slinking into a corner past a few sullen-looking men at the bare tables. The innkeeper waited to see if we had money before he reluctantly brought each of us a piece of bread and a glass of wine. "That's all," he declared. "First the Belgians, then the ones from the north, then the Parisians, now you. It's too much."

The bottles behind the bar were empty, but here too a radio stood between them. It was turned on, but we heard only babbling voices and then, suddenly, the "Marseillaise." Nobody stood up. The innkeeper turned the dial. "You can't tell any more what you're getting," he said. "Most of the time it's the *boches*." The local French station had been dismantled and was transmitting only off and on from a hideout, he said, switching back to the "Marseillaise."

It had become louder. "*Le jour de gloire est arrivé.*" We heard the crackling of static and, through the static, scraps of a newscast: "Tours bombed again . . . only light damage. . . . The government at Bordeaux. . . . "

Static. Dead silence. We waited while the innkeeper fumbled with the set. Suddenly another voice, clear, distinct, without any interference: "Marshal Pétain has concluded an armistice with the Führer."

Everyone jumped to his feet. Glasses clinked; rejoicing broke out: "*La paix, nous voulons la paix. . . .* We—want—

peace," the men shouted, drumming the beat with their fists on the tabletops.

The innkeeper had vanished. The radio was jubilantly blaring the "Marseillaise" again as the cellar door opened and a small keg appeared, our host beneath it. He pulled the plug and began to draw glass after glass. *"Marchons, marchons,"* blared the radio, but nobody paid attention. *"Qu'un sang impur abreuve nos sillons."*

At the bar, in front of the radio, the innkeeper's wife was opening a bundle. Where had she found it so quickly? Loaves of bread were rolling out of it, a large round cheese, a long sausage. We had a feast, attacking the piles of food and emptying glasses that were refilled as by magic.

"Attention, attention," the radio screamed. Willy-nilly, we stopped to listen. "Frenchmen, you've heard the order of the day: They shall not pass! . . . Our troops are fighting bravely. . . . Help is on its way from England, from America. . . . *Vive la République!"*

"Merde!" The man's voice split the silence. Fists shook in rage; the innkeeper grabbed the radio and shoved it into a corner. Then the lights went out.

By the time we could see in the semidarkness, our table was bare again. Food, wine, everything, had disappeared— also from the other tables. Quarrels broke out, and we quickly left the inn and headed south once more.

"Bordeaux," said Walter. "We must get to a port—to a ship—we have to get to Bordeaux," he insisted, but we were a long way from that last glimmer of hope.

Only fear made me go on. We tried to avoid the towns; they might be targets for destruction. We were crisscrossing a dying country, passing through eerie villages whose names I never knew. The houses along our road seemed like stage props. Doors shut in our faces when we knocked, asking for food. Here and there a bakery might yield an old roll or two—after hours of waiting outside.

150

Somewhere we got a tin of tomato paste and licked it out like stray dogs. We drank water from farmyard wells, and now and then we were lucky enough to hitch a ride on an ox cart or a hay wagon. Sometimes we were allowed to sleep in a barn rather than in a ditch, and it felt good to stretch our sore limbs in the hay. We could not rest, though, could not linger even if given the chance, with the same words spreading, whipping us on everywhere: "The Germans are coming." They were behind us, ahead of us, around us—were we running away from the Germans or right into their hands? By this time we did not know.

Two weeks of flight lay behind us when we reached the Garonne. Once again a bridge led to a crossroads: One sign, marked "BORDEAUX, 15 KILOMÈTRES," pointed downriver, more or less northwest; the other said "BAYONNE, 250 KILOMÈTRES," and the road seemed to lead due south. We stood in between. In between, somewhere to the south, the Garonne ran into the Lot—or the other way round; I remembered that much. Not far to the west of us must be the sea, the dunes of Arcachon, where I had spent those stolen hours, long since run out with the departure of two trains in opposite directions. . . . Now it was Walter and I who had to choose between opposite directions, and again my choice was south.

Walter favored Bordeaux. It was just a few miles, after all, and we must find a ship before it was too late.

And what if it was too late now? If no more ships sailed? If the Germans were in Bordeaux?

Having no one to advise us, we flipped a coin. Heads meant Bordeaux, Walter decreed; if it came up tails, we would go south. I threw the sou piece into the air. It spun to the pavement, rolled in a circle, wobbled, fell. We ran to look: It was tails.

A car passed, heading for Bordeaux. We stood looking after it. Had the oracle deceived us? A southbound car whizzed past, and Walter signaled frantically—too late. The car was gone.

"You try," Walter suggested. "A woman is more appealing." I posted myself in the middle of the road. Something like an arrow suddenly flew at me, swerving at the last moment. Brakes screeched, and when I straightened up in a cloud of dust, I saw a luxury car with two French officers sticking their heads out the windows to stare back at me.

My hands rose in supplication. "*Amenez nous*—take us, help us!"

The door of the low-slung limousine opened, and a uniformed arm waved impatiently at the empty rear seats. We jumped in, the door slammed, and we were off—to Bayonne or at least in the direction of Bayonne, in headlong flight from Bordeaux.

Ahead, the Route Nationale stretched in endless desolation. Bombed-out villages rushed past at ninety miles an hour. We were speeding south through a wasteland, and in the sky torn clouds raced along with us into the dusk. In two hours we got farther than in the whole two weeks before.

At another crossroads, as hastily as they had picked us up at the Garonne, the officers let us out. The lights that we saw, they told us, were the outskirts of Bayonne. Their car made a sharp turn off the highway and vanished in the dark.

We couldn't go wrong this time; there were still street lamps burning in Bayonne. We simply followed them. The sky was black. What began as a drizzle became a cloudburst that drove us to the shelter of a streetcar stop, where shadowy figures sat on a bench beneath the tin roof, talking in an unintelligible language. One of them rose and came toward us. "*Qui est là?* Who's there?" he asked, and then he suddenly flung out his arms: "Mehring! Where do you come from?"

They embraced, and I recognized the Polish writer—what was his name? He was a friend of Roth's and the author of *Salt of the Earth*—yes, it was Joseph Wittlin. We sat down together. He had reached Bayonne in a Polish convoy. As soon as the rain subsided, he said, we would have to move on; the Germans were coming, but two British ships were said to be still in the port of Bayonne, waiting for Polish soldiers. "Come along. Let's try our luck."

The storm did not subside. Through rain and wind, groping our way along the houses, we reached the harbor. Never before had I seen foam so white on waves so black. A single giant water mass was rolling toward us. The fishing boats lay as though spewed ashore, covered with dripping nets and ropes that stretched like tentacles. On the pier a multitude surged back and forth, and riding at anchor in the outer harbor was one ship, a dark shadow, bowing her masts to the storm.

Crazily swaying small boats shuttled between the pier and the ship. They took only military personnel. Military police with crossed bayonets formed a barrier, pushing back women and other civilians trying to break through. Supervising the proceedings, somewhat to one side, was a tall figure: the British captain in gold-braided Navy uniform, ramrod-straight, unmoving. He never turned his head; only his bright blue eyes followed the boats on their way to his ship and back.

A few soldiers' wives fell on their knees before him, pleading for permission to accompany their men to England. Not a muscle twitched in the captain's face; his only answer, delivered in a perfectly calm voice, was the one word "Sorry." Then the blue eyes turned to the M.P.'s, and they pulled the women to their feet and drove them back behind the barrier.

I used the moment of confusion to approach the captain. He did not seem to see me until I addressed him: "Please. . . ."

The ice-cold eyes silenced me, but the voice was friendly: "Are you British?"

I could only shake my head.

"Sorry," it came back. No shrug, no gesture, compassionate or otherwise—"Sorry." It rang like a death sentence.

I thought of jumping into the water—too late: Some of the Polish women had just plunged in, trying to swim after the boats, and the boats were turning back only to form a new barrier. The women were hauled out and brought ashore, and around us the ring of police tightened. All hope died.

The storm died down at last at daybreak, when the captain left in the last boat, and the ship weighed anchor with the fog lifting from a calm sea.

What are we waiting for? I asked myself. We stood on the pier, Wittlin, Mehring, and I, looking after the ship until it seemed to dissolve in the blue haze between sky and water, until everything out there was blue like the British captain's eyes, which I have never forgotten.

I don't remember exactly when we got the news. We had tried to buy poison in Bayonne to keep us out of the hands of the Germans, but there was no poison to be had without a prescription. We were sitting in a waterfront bistro, each with a glass of wine, when a couple of sailors came in. They knew all about it. The British ship, they told us, had struck a mine and gone down with all hands. No survivors.

Next morning the first German motorcycle patrols were said to have been sighted somewhere in Bayonne. There were no French ports to the south of us anymore; we were almost at the Spanish border. Although Spain belonged to Franco, Hitler's friend, and we heard that the border was as tightly guarded as the British ship had been, it looked like our last hope. A truckload of Poles—alive because they had missed the ship—had the same idea, and Wittlin persuaded them to take us along.

We set out along the sea road, but at St. Jean-de-Luz the truck ran out of gas. The Poles vainly tried to find some in the elegant resort; the fuel picture on the "Silver Coast" was as bleak as between Paris and Étampes. The street picture differed strikingly. We met people with beach bags, on their way to swim in the ocean; shops were open, and cafés as crowded as at Arcachon last August, before the crisis. We could not believe our eyes. A picture of peace.

We sat down at a café table, not noticing the startled faces roundabout. "Coffee," Walter said, "they've got coffee." They had fresh croissants too, with butter, marmalade, and honey. We were in Paradise, saved from the Flood. I felt transported back to Clairac, and for the moment, sipping the hot, fragrant elixir of life, I refused to think that this paradise would not last either.

I had my third or fourth croissant in my mouth when someone tugged at my arm. "Pauli," a lady with a large beach hat said in a voice full of sympathy, "what has happened to you? You look terrible." And in a whisper she added, "Can I lend you some money?"

I stared at the beach hat and finally recognized an old friend of mine underneath it, Gertrud Kanitz, an actress from Berlin. "Thanks," I said, confused, and produced the bank notes we hadn't been able to get a crust of bread for. "We can pay."

She was greeting Mehring by then, explaining that she was here on vacation with Rudi. I knew Rudi; in Berlin he had been a movie agent. Nothing had happened to them, my friend said. And where had we come from?

I had to think about that, but before I found the answer, Mehring said, "From Paris."

"Oh, I see." She understood. In Paris there were the Germans—in Bordeaux too, according to reports. But now the armistice was in effect at last, despite the speeches broadcast against it by the British and a general named De Gaulle, who had been in the subcabinet and had fled to London. "Here we're safe," said the actress, "behind the line of demarcation."

We mentioned the tales of German patrols in Bayonne, but she assured us that those must have been idle rumors. She urged me to come to her hotel, to wash up and change in her room—didn't I realize that my skirt was in tatters? Mehring could try to get us a room in the meantime; with the hotels so full, it would not be easy.

Mehring was agreeable. Then it occurred to him that there might be an American consul at St. Jean-de-Luz—in Bayonne everything had been shut down. "I'll find out and meet you here," he said.

I went with the actress. For weeks I had forgotten about my appearance, but now I felt ashamed of my torn skirt. I did not possess another. My blouse was filthy too. I stopped at a shop to buy a suit; it suddenly helped to have some money left. When I came back to the café, Walter gave me an astonished look—I seemed changed, apparently—before blurting out the latest disaster.

The American consul was in town but would see no one, and people claimed to have heard that he had thrown away all passports and papers entrusted to him. *"Qu'est-ce qu'on fait?"* Mehring asked. "What are we going to do?"

"I'm going to the hairdresser's," I said. My hair was a mess, and I would not be swayed from my purpose. I hadn't been to a beauty parlor since Paris—disgraceful.

My new bob was still under the dryer when Mehring burst in. "You're going to kill us with your beauty parlor!" he screamed. "I just heard the radio: the whole coast will be occupied—the last bus is just leaving—come—"

He threw the hairdresser's money at him and pulled me out into the street. He sprinted ahead, and I ran after him with my hair still wet; we caught the bus by a whisker. It went inland, bound for Oloron and the Hautes-Pyrénées, and once again Walter and I were alone, wedged among fleeing strangers. We wondered if the happy-go-lucky "vacationers" in St. Jean-de-Luz would be able to scatter. We wondered about Wittlin and his Poles. Had they found gasoline to get away?

It was night when the bus made its last stop. We got off to find gendarmes waiting. They rounded us up and herded us into an "assembly center," a large shed with mattresses on the floor, where we were to spend the night. The word was that in the morning we would continue on our way.

In the morning we found we were prisoners. The side doors were locked, and a gendarme posted at the front door said we had to stay put until the arrival of another bus, which would take us to a place of safety. Hours passed. Penned in, we waited for our "transportation." Walter and I had no valid papers at all—what would happen to us? All these weeks of running and scrambling and starving, only to be caught here in the end, like mice in a trap.

After three anxious hours I made a chance discovery. Way back in a corner of the shed, half hidden by trash, a little door was ajar. No one else had seen it yet. Mehring stood in front of me, waiting like the rest. I gently tugged at his sleeve, and when he turned his head, I pressed a finger to my lips before pointing furtively to the open back door.

Slowly, soundlessly, we stole along the wall to the door, out through the gap into a dark corridor, toward a glimmer of light at the end, round a corner, round another corner. Faster and faster we walked, ran, changed directions, as if we had to throw off pursuers; but there were no pursuers. No one except ourselves had seen the exit. Not till later did it strike me how greatly the mousetrap with the small unnoticed back door resembled the big prison that was France.

Being chased by the Germans had become a habit, but now we had to learn again to dodge the French police as well. As in Clairac once upon a time, it was illegal for us to move from place to place without a safe conduct, so we could not afford to be caught again. We kept away from the main highways, traveled by side roads, and stayed in the mountain region that was less likely to be occupied.

Once, following the sound of church bells, we got into a

procession bound for Lourdes. It had to do with the armistice. One knew that it divided France into an occupied and an unoccupied zone, but no border line had been announced as yet; all the talk about it was guesswork, a woman told us, but St. Bernadette had stopped the Germans once before. "We'll ask her to do it again."

We fell in with the pilgrims. Together we walked behind Bernadette's image, but there was no room for us in their tents when they camped at Lourdes. Aimlessly we strolled through the narrow streets. No hotel, no hostel, no lodging house, had any vacancies. Most food shops were closed; the new government of Marshal Pétain had commandeered almost all foodstuffs. This was bad, people said, but at least the marshal had made peace and the few fools who wanted to fight on had left, gone to join the crazy British. They'd soon find out that nobody could resist the Germans.

We felt wholly forsaken. Without meaning to, we entered a small shop selling religious objects—by then we were accustomed to following St. Bernadette. In the window there, she was on her knees, life-size, and looking at us kindly out of open books; inside, a heavyset man stood thumbing through one of the books. When we came in, he looked up and came forward to embrace us. Little Bernadette had led us to Franz Werfel.

"We're walking in her steps," he said almost apologetically. He was studying her story, preparing to write his famous novel. His wife, Alma, was nearby, in the hotel where they had managed to find a room—or a hole, rather, a sort of *cachot* not unlike the abandoned jail in which Bernadette Soubirous had grown up a century ago. Werfel bought a book, I a couple of amulets. Then the three of us went to join Alma, who hailed us effusively and declared that only a miracle had saved us all.

The news of the German breakthrough had surprised the Werfels in Sanary, on the Riviera. After Paris fell, they had traveled to Bordeaux, trusting in the French government not to let the Germans get there; when this faith turned out to be misplaced, they had fled south by taxi, and we figured out that we and they must have been in St. Jean-de-Luz at the same time. They too had left there on June 26, again by taxi, and had remained in Lourdes until now, the middle of July.

Every bed, sofa, and bathtub in their Hôtel Vatican was taken, but Alma's persuasiveness won out: The proprietor let Walter and me spend the night lying on the billiard table in the bar. We were still up there, resting our sore bones, when the Werfels returned from their morning pilgrimage to the grotto of Massabielle. Alma explained that the spot where the Virgin had appeared to Bernadette, had a healing effect on her soul and that the water from the miraculous spring was good both for her and for Franzl. Sometimes they went twice a day.

Mehring came along only on the walks we took around Lourdes. It was a picturesque place, and to visualize the saint one really did not need to go to the grotto; there were innumerable little Bernadettes all over town, with their kerchiefs and their blue sashes of the "Children of Mary." As Mehring saw it, those little French provincial saints all looked alike.

Werfel shook his head. He knew only the one Bernadette who once told a skeptical prelate: "The Lady said to tell you what I saw; she didn't tell me to make you believe it." It was hard to tell whether Werfel himself did or did not believe in the apparitions, but it was plain how seriously he took the vow that he had made for Alma's sake: If they lived, if they were brought safely through the massacre, he'd tell the story of the miracle of Lourdes as it appeared to him. He would write *The Song of Bernadette*.

"Despoiled but for the miracle"—this was how Lourdes appeared to Walter Mehring. He remained the optimistic skeptic, the doubter who believed in something that to me

seemed as improbable as any miracle: He thought the cable
we had sent to Thomas Mann might save us yet; I thought
that even if an answer had been sent, it would never reach us.
We talked to the Werfels about what to do. They were
moving to a better room in the hotel and offered to arrange
for us to get their *cachot*, but there was no rest for Walter.

Having cabled "in the name of us all," he argued, we must
seek an answer in behalf of us all. If there was one, it could
only be found at an American consulate. In Toulouse, perhaps. The Werfels could not walk there, but we could. They
had to stay with Bernadette until trains were running again,
but we must get going.

It was no pilgrimage that swallowed us up this time; it
was a column of army trucks carrying soldiers to Toulouse
for demobilization. "*La guerre est finie*," they cried. The roadside was strewn with discarded rifles. Some Czech soldiers
gave us a lift. They looked more battered than the French;
when the German tanks broke through, they said, they had
been thrown right into their path, to plug the holes, and
had taken heavy casualties. I thought of Passer. Then I heard
that surviving officers had been evacuated to England, where
Czech resistance would go on.

Toulouse looked like a vast disintegrating army camp.
Senegalese and other colonial troops marched through the
streets, the only units with a semblance of order. The
American Consulate was closed, the city hall besieged by
masses of soldiers and civilians. Its pink stone walls were
covered with slips of paper fluttering in the breeze like
countless flags of surrender.

Everyone in Toulouse seemed to be looking for someone.
Refugees from all directions, discharged soldiers in the most
varied uniforms—all of them put up their names and addresses
on the walls of the city hall. So did we. Suddenly somebody called my name. It was Hans Natonek. He had arrived
before us, also with a Czech unit. We asked him about Weiss,

the fourth man in our Parisian horror play—and this was when we learned that Ernst Weiss was dead.

Only we three surviving signers of the cable were reunited. We asked Natonek where he was staying, but he wasn't staying anywhere; he had spent last night walking the streets. Another futile hunt for lodgings began, and when we finally rested at a bistro, tired and discouraged, Mehring struck up a conversation with the *patronne*, about this and that, before coming out with the question: "Do you happen to know of a room, madame? Anything, anywhere—we have money," he importuned the woman, and I had to think of the dead soldier's bed before Orléans.

"*Ah, ça.*" She shrugged. There were no sleeping quarters in Toulouse, not for any money. People slept on park benches and under bridges until the *flics* chased them away.

Natonek sat staring glumly at his glass. Mehring persisted: "A cellar, perhaps?"

The woman seemed to think of something. Then she shook her head. "You don't want to go there."

"Yes, we do. Where is it? Tell us, madame, I beg of you—"

She made the sign of the cross. "It's the garret of the late curé, God rest his poor soul," she whispered as though afraid to broach the subject. The priest had died there years ago. Of syphilis. But he came back every night. "He haunts the place, you know."

We did not leave without getting the address from her. It was not far, and the tavern-keeper's greetings plus a hundred-franc note soon elicited the key from the concierge. We had to go upstairs by ourselves, though; she wouldn't set foot in the place, she said in a firm tone.

The stairs creaked and the rusty lock took minutes to open, but eventually we got in. The place was like a junk heap, with plaster all over the floor and gaping holes in the roof; when I drew back the tattered curtains, I nearly cut myself on the jagged remnant of a windowpane. In a corner we

161

found a dust-covered pile of mattresses beside a washstand. It was evident that for a long time nobody had set foot in the haunted garret; the Werfels' *cachot* seemed a luxury suite in comparison.

When we reappeared at the concierge's, she assumed that we had seen enough and wanted our money back; it came as a pleasant surprise to her that we only asked for clean blankets. Supplied with a few army blankets, we climbed back upstairs. It was getting dark, and the only light we had was a flashlight of Natonek's. We spread the mattresses, wrapped ourselves in the blankets, and went to sleep.

I woke up suddenly. It was dark. Across the street a clock was striking, but I thought I had been awakened by a different sound. The clock struck twelve, and in the moonlight between the torn curtains I saw a dark round head, with glistening eyes, in the window. I screamed. The flashlight went on, lit up the window—and a big black cat disappeared into the night.

Night after night, punctually at the witching hour, the cat reappeared. He did not bother us but merely looked in and departed. Could it be the spirit of the late curé? We got quite used to him, and Walter sketched his silhouette on the new slip of paper we put on the city hall with our address. To make the slip more noticeable I hung an amulet from Lourdes beside it, a small silver medal of the Blessed Virgin. It could do no harm.

One evening, a sound awakened us long before midnight. We sat up, all three of us—was the poor curé early? The sound came from the door, though, not from the window. Someone was knocking, too gently for police. Full of misgivings, I went to open it.

Before me in the flashlight beam stood a *prestataire* with his knapsack. "Carli!" I cried.

He had my holy medal with him, and Walter's slip of paper. He had just arrived in Toulouse, and like everyone else he had gone straight to the city hall to search the fluttering pieces of paper on the pink walls. In the morning he would have to report to his unit, but now he could stay with us. There was so much to tell that we kept talking till the break of dawn—Walter and I more than Carli, whose experiences had in the main been limited to labor on defense works that were senseless because no defense was made. We were so glad to be together again that it struck us only the next day: The black cat had not come that night. Carli saw it only on paper.

In the morning he obtained his proper discharge papers. As for back pay, the clerk at the demobilization office declared that for *prestataires* there wasn't any. Sadly Carli showed his empty purse: When he turned it upside down, nothing but the little medal of the Virgin of Lourdes rolled tinkling over the counter. "*Voilà.*"

The woman looked perplexed. Then she resolutely reached into a drawer and took out a bundle of bills. "We'll just make an exception," she said, handing Carli the money together with his little silver Virgin.

The miracles continued. On the same day we were able to buy railway tickets to Marseilles: The first train would leave Toulouse that afternoon. Natonek and Mehring agreed that in Marseilles we were sure to find the American Consulate open.

I said I was going to Clairac. "No," said Carli. "I don't know how I survived that the last time. You're coming with us."

This time I had to give in. Carli was convinced that with his discharge papers he could give some protection to Mehring and me. Natonek had a valid Czech passport and was fairly safe anyway, though he was not supposed to travel without a safe conduct either. The thousands waiting at the Toulouse railway station made it easy to get lost in the throng, however. On our way to the track I dropped a postcard to Clairac into a mailbox—a sign of life "en route to Marseilles." I could give no address. This, I believe, was my first word to Gilbert since leaving Paris. (Walter Mehring still maintains, however, that I did write to Clairac before this, from every stop we made, long before trains resumed running.)

On the trip we stood for hours, wedged in the aisle. No conductor could get through, which made us feel better. We were on the train all right, but how we were going to get off remained a puzzle. There would be a gate, a ticket-taker, and police all over the station, as likely as not. The decision came closer and closer; we were already passing through the outskirts of Marseilles. I saw Carli push his way to a door, and I pushed after him without asking any questions, the others after me. On a hillside the train stopped at a switch signal.

"Get off," Carli called back, opened the door, and jumped.

Mehring and I followed. Natonek stayed on the train; it was beginning to move again. Later we heard that in Marseilles one could avoid the police by simply walking through the railroad restaurant and out onto the street.

We ran away from the tracks and down the hillside toward the sea. One of the little suburbs of Marseilles lay ahead of us. Mehring thinks he remembers taking a streetcar; I believe we reached the fishing village on foot. Its name was Pointe Rouge.

We went into a small bar on the road that ran along the beach. At a table of fishermen sat a bearded man whom Mehring suddenly recognized, although they had not seen each other for a long time. Emil Gumbel, professor of statistics and a pacifist of international renown, had emigrated already from the Weimar Republic; now he had fled from Lyons, abandoning his university chair and growing a beard so as not to be recognized by Nazi agents. That Mehring knew him right away upset the professor.

"You can't be too cautious," he whispered to us. "The Gestapo is all over Marseilles. Here in the Bar Mistral it's relatively safe, but there's no way to get out."

So there we sat together, and we stayed with Gumbel at the Bar Mistral—in the mousetrap.

CHAPTER 9

The Answer

The United States Consulate in Marseilles looked like a castle. A flight of broad marble steps swept up to the front entrance, and the huge park around the building in the suburb of Montredon ran all the way to the seashore, with a mountain landscape as backdrop. The park was overgrown, and close to the steps the beech trees spread their boughs to keep the July heat off the loiterers who stood or sat there or leaned on the balustrade day after day, like beggars waiting for alms to be passed out by the lord of the manor.

They were refugees, of course, from a variety of German-ruled or German-conquered nations; they were not beggars. Or were they, this tired-looking lot without rights or claims, hanging on the grace of unknown institutions, on the goodwill of unknown persons, waiting for alms that money could not buy? And we among them. . . .

It was to beg that we were there, even if the admission we

sought was not to the castle. The castle stood for a dream. In our dreams, in the dreams of all these fugitives from the ever-widening range of Hitler's power, the white steps in the outskirts of Marseilles led to the Promised Land.

To give pause to any who might be tempted to rush it the portal atop the steps was guarded by a doorman and three signs. The first large sign, in English and French, read: "APPLICATIONS FROM CENTRAL EUROPE CLOSED." The second sign read: "QUOTA TRANSFERS FROM PARIS DISCONTINUED." The third sign read: "PASSAGE FROM LISBON SOLD OUT FOR MONTHS."

We got the message. "All hope abandon"—the device of Dante's Hell was emblazoned on these Pearly Gates in triplicate.

The beeches rustled, and from a distance came the soothing roll of the waves, but our ears rang with sounds from hell. We were hounded by rumors. Tomorrow or next week Marseilles would be occupied. . . . An application for a permit to stay would be a ticket to a concentration camp. . . . The Gestapo was at the Prefecture now, looking for us. . . .

The circle of our friends that had shrunk in Paris was swiftly growing again. The entire refugee mass squeezed itself into the bottleneck of Marseilles. They came from internment camps and out of "unarmed military labor service" and from country hideouts. Many would not tell where they lived in Marseilles, but there was no need to make appointments. On the white steps of Montredon, sooner or later, you met them all. All, that is, who had made it.

We did not know what had become of our cable to Thomas Mann. We had signed it "in the name of us all," in the name of all our scattered friends and colleagues, and after four weeks no word for all or any of us had reached the Consulate. Perhaps the cable had never arrived in the first place. In the chaotic final days of Paris it was more likely than not to have ended up in a wastebasket, as we had ended up in this port without exit. Considering the kind of censorship to which

168

all communications were now subject, we did not dare send another cable to the United States.

At the American Consulate we met Heinrich Mann, Thomas Mann's brother, kindly and a little cumbersome of movement in his seventieth year. Asked if he had not heard anything from America either, he would shake his head with an indulgent, older-brotherly smile. "That's the way Thomas is," he would say—and like an echo from the pit some barbed comment would be added by Lion Feuchtwanger, his constant companion.

Sometimes we met an attractive man whose name was not spoken aloud; his natural charm and unnatural reserve seemed hard to reconcile unless you knew he was Konrad Heiden, Hitler's biographer and the one writer the Führer hated most. One day we met the novelist Leonhard Frank, who had barely climbed over the barbed-wire fence of his internment camp before the Germans reached it. He brought news of Walter Hasenclever: when the Germans approached the camp he was in, the playwright had killed himself.

Frank had no place to stay, so we suggested that he hide with us. The Bar Mistral was full, but Mehring had a second bed in his room next door; Frank moved in with him and joined us on the visits to the Consulate which had become our daily routine. Routine helps; routine gets you through things you could not bear otherwise. It was a pleasant morning stroll along the beach and then uphill, a bit inland. When we had by chance found our quiet little haven, we had no idea that it was in walking distance of the spot to which we looked for salvation. It had been enough to know then that Pointe Rouge was outside the raiding range of the Marseilles Prefecture. Neither Mehring nor I had valid papers left; whenever we ventured into the city, Carli tagged along so there would be at least one presentable document between the three of us, the *prestataire* discharge he had received at the demobilization of the unarmed labor corps. The last installment of his army pay, drawn at the same time, was also shared with us.

The Cannebière was colorful as ever; it took a close look to note the changes on Marseilles's famed main street. The seamen who used to crowd it had been replaced by discharged soldiers. A bright costume had once marked a man as being from the colonies, in France on business or for pleasure; now it indicated the colonial army unit he was stranded with. One saw Moroccans, Spahis with black silk sashes, turbaned Senegalese. And instead of tourists from all over the world, there were the refugees—Parisians and other northerners, Belgians, and such as we.

Our main effort was to go unnoticed, to blend into the crowd, to be mistaken for Belgians or Frenchmen from the north, if possible. Our colleagues with Polish, Czech, or other passports did not have this problem—not Wittlin, who had known of the ship in Bayonne but here could not find one; not the Werfels, who felt safe enough to stay at their usual Grand Hôtel de Louvre et de la Paix; least of all Dr. Gumbel, a naturalized Frenchman due to his professorship at Lyons. Gumbel was in perfect order with the French; only the Germans were apt to arrest him on sight, and the rumors of a Gestapo presence in Marseilles kept him at Pointe Rouge, away from the bustling city.

The port, always so busy, showed few signs of life. Out beyond the mole ocean liners and large freighters rode somnolently at anchor, and the small ships that were packed into the Vieux Port, the Old Harbor at the foot of the Cannebière, looked like a mothball fleet. Only the fishing boats would still go out and return to empty their nets at the dockside, where the screeching fishwives had their stands, where lobsters and crabs tried desperately to crawl out of baskets before being boiled alive in pots over a coal fire, as usual.

You could buy them for a few sous and eat them on the

spot, wrapped in old newspapers. They were as fresh as could be, and we were hungry; but somehow they did not taste as good as usual. I kept thinking of a quip by Ferenc Molnar. Years back, in Vienna, the Hungarian playwright had explained to us why Jews were like lobsters: "The pot is boiling, but until the lid is on, they think they can get out."

Was the lid on? No one knew. The port and the U.S. Consulate had drawn us all to Marseilles—were both of them paralyzed? We had yet to see a smoke plume on the horizon. The breakwaters looked like walls built to immure us. We saw the rock overlooking the Vieux Port, and there, on the top, was Notre Dame de la Garde, standing watch over Marseilles as she had done for centuries—far longer than Our Lady of the Grotto at Lourdes, where Franz Werfel had vowed that, if rescued, he would tell the tale of little Bernadette. He too was here, still waiting to be rescued, waiting like all the rest of us in Marseilles where Our Lady of the Guard kept silent watch over a port from which no ship sailed.

Today the Vieux Port is gone. It was blown to bits by the Germans before the liberation of the city. Notre Dame de la Garde, untouched as ever, is still watching over Marseilles.

We were cut off from the world and from the truth. Passing by hotels or cafés, we heard the radio blaring marches or propaganda for the "New Order." What newspapers there were got their news from Dr. Goebbels, directly or indirectly. Sometimes they enabled you to draw conclusions. When they announced that Pétain's government had moved from Bordeaux to Vichy, for instance, you reasoned that the Germans would stay in Bordeaux but would not go to Vichy. With the armistice terms still unpublished, there was no telling where the Germans would halt, if anywhere. As for refugees, there was never a word about refugees in the papers.

The rumors made up for it. We lived trying to look like everyone else and to avoid close contact with anyone else, but between us and the world lay a tangled web of rumors, fresh or stale or conflicting—take your pick. Facts emerged slowly; one of the first was that we could not get an exit visa.

At the consulates in the city, lines kept forming anyway, with the Portuguese and Spanish most beleaguered. No one thought of lingering in the land of Hitler's ally Franco, but the Spaniards could give a transit visa that would at least let you pass through—provided you already possessed a visa to Portugal. And Portugal was regarded as the one relatively safe refuge in Europe, which was why the Portuguese gave no more than a transit visa either—provided, of course, you could show that you would be admitted somewhere overseas.

As in a vicious circle we chased from pillar to post, only to end up on the steps of our dream castle. We hardly ever went in. We knew now that only the visa division of the consulate was housed at Montredon; people who had blundered into the main office in downtown Marseilles told of being ushered out fast. "That's for Americans," they reported. The visa division was ruled by the vice-consul, whose name was Harry Bingham. We did not wish to disturb Mr. Bingham, since the signs outside said he could do nothing for us—unless, perhaps, we were to get an answer to our cable.

A few times I ventured as far as the Louis XV desk of Mr. Bingham's secretary. She spoke French, and having told me in English that there was nothing for me, she would make sure by repeating: *"Rien pour vous."* She also had a memory for faces, and after my second or third call I no longer needed to stand in corners with the antique vases if the velvet benches were occupied; she would shake her head at me as soon as I came in. Now and then I saw a beggar or two sent upstairs, all aglow—most of these lucky ones had been farsighted enough to send their parents or children to America in time to have by now become Americans themselves.

We preferred to wait outdoors. As a rule we wrote our names on a slip of paper each morning and gave this to the doorman. He would take it in, and after a couple of hours he would bring it back, shaking his head like the secretary.

More facts emerged. The line of demarcation became known: We were officially in the "unoccupied zone," of whose establishment we heard with mixed emotions. We felt relief, of course. Should we? Would Hitler have left half of France to the French unless he thought it would help him? Not many resolved this moral dilemma as easily as Alma Werfel, who decided that it must have been Pétain who had "stood up" to Hitler. "So the old goat was good for something after all," she said.

By the end of July it was evident that the marshal had not been too vigorous in standing up. From journalists and others with reliable sources of information we heard at last what the armistice said about us. The French government, it turned out, had obliged itself to "surrender on demand" all Germans named by the Reich and to prevent their flight abroad.

"Germans" meant all those called Germans by the Reich. It meant all of us. It meant all the ones we called Germans: Mann and Frank, as well as Mehring and Feuchtwanger—for once, the Reich deigned to designate Jews as Germans. It meant Carli and me, because Austria was now the "German Ostmark." It meant Franz Werfel, a native of Prague and a holder of a Czechoslovak passport, because Czechoslovakia was now the "German Protectorate Bohemia and Moravia." It meant Wittlin, the Pole, because Poland was now a German "Government General."

The French were supposed to hold the lid on us and serve us up to order; Molnar in Vienna had not known how apt his lobster simile would be in France. Specifically, we were to be kept from getting out of the pot. Hence the exit visas.

Besides the police of Marseilles, among its variegated crowds a new civilian type was now seen more and more

often, unmistakably German and with a quality that made
your spine tingle, a quality that all of us knew, though no
one could define it. The Gestapo was in town. A new crop
of rumors sprouted: that the roundup had begun, that so-and-
so and such-and-such had disappeared. Two German Socialist leaders, Rudolf Breitscheid and Rudolf Hilferding, were
widely believed to be missing—until someone saw them
again at their usual café. Another rumor proved true, although
the Nazis were probably not to blame: Willi Münzenberg, a
veteran German Communist who had openly denounced the
Stalin-Hitler pact, had been found dead on the route of his
flight from Paris, not shot but hung from a tree.

And mixed with the whispers of tragedy were timid ones
of rescue chances: of passports for sale, of smuggler trails
across the Pyrenees, of ships leaving port, unseen, on foggy
nights. On such nights the five of us at Pointe Rouge would
sit together in my attic room. The window was no larger
than a bull's-eye; the fog outside and the sound of the sea
made us feel as if we were in a ship's cabin, except for the
solid floor. Little Walter Mehring used to sit slightly
hunched over, his back to the sea—as George Grosz, long
before the Reichstag fire, had prophetically painted him
against a background of Berlin in flames. Facing him across
my wobbly table sat Leonhard Frank, looking like an old
woodcut. His white hair and incredibly blue eyes gleamed,
even though only one dingy bulb lit the room. By its dim
light Frank was working ceaselessly on a new novel, to be
called *A Long Life with You, a Long Life*.

The title may have served to distract him from the fact of
our numbered days. He did not seem distracted by our
company: He sought it night after night. Perhaps his fears
grew when he was alone.

Mehring too kept musing and jotting down verses, and the
rest of us would wait in silence for one of the two to feel like
reading aloud. It was very still during those nights. The

174

bar below, where the fishermen drank their aperitifs in the daytime, had closed hours earlier. The fishermen took their small boats out at dawn and had no time for night life.

I too, all by myself, kept working on my novel about Clairac, the village where for a time I had thought of becoming a French peasant girl and had been arrested as a spy instead. All through the flight I too had been lugging a half-finished manuscript along with my few other possessions.

Frank's piercing eyes were on me. "Why don't you read something, Hertha?" A master spoke; I obeyed. I started reading a passage that took me back to the old stone bridge over the Lot River, but no one there seemed to be really listening.

"There was night music in the waves," I read, "forms dissolving between light and shadow. The stone balustrade under my hands suddenly was in the Vienna Woods; I had only to hold out my arms to touch the branches."

"Just a moment," Frank broke in. "That's not a bad line." I blushed for joy. Frank used to put down lines like building blocks; he carved them, so to speak, and then placed them slowly one upon another as if each page were a house in which the reader might make himself at home. No doubt, Leonhard Frank was a master of the German language. A Franconian cobbler's son with no more than a grade-school education, he had taught it to himself by infinite effort, but the acquisition of this mastery appeared to have exhausted his linguistic powers. He was incapable of learning any other language, not even a phrase of one. The impediment this constituted on a flight through France could well be imagined.

Mehring, on the other hand, spoke French as fluently as he spoke German, and without a trace of an accent. He and I were alive only because we had always managed to pass for a French couple. Yet even in Paris, the home of his choice, Mehring had confessed that now and then he dreamed in Berlinese. . . .

175

A flashlight speared the fog outside, and down in the bar a door creaked. Frank gave a start; he always thought he was about to be arrested. "Mehring, go see what's the matter," he whispered.

"Nonsense." Mehring did not even look up from his works. "They are after fish, not after you."

Frank fixed the little poet with an icy stare. "You wouldn't feel like joking," he said, "if you were as endangered as I am."

That did it. "I," Mehring screamed without the least fear of listeners, "I was personally expatriated—stripped of my German citizenship as an individual, on one of Goebbels's first lists!" It was his proudest boast.

"And I"—Frank was still keeping his voice down—"I left of my own free will. As a so-called Aryan I would have needed only to change my tune."

"*Voilà*," spat Mehring, white with rage. "There you have it!"

Forgetting himself, Frank pounded the table. "I have my convictions! Over there they hate that more than any-thing——"

Mehring, half the other's size, closed in. "They've hated me a lot longer," he sneered.

We others in the audience were trying hard not to smile; such battles took place daily, and if the cause was not one thing, it was another. Dr. Gumbel thought it might help to pour the oil of literary history on the raging waters. "A hundred years ago it was Heine and Börne," he said, "who used to fight for the title of 'most wanted.' "

Instantly the battlers joined against him. "You talk of examples? You have a French passport!"

"But everyone knows who I am," Gumbel said loftily. It was why he had grown a full beard—to avoid recognition. The beard was becoming, moreover, and Gumbel knew it. "Anyhow, now we are all on one list," he said soothingly. "All in the same boat."

Out on Pointe Rouge we could hear the fishing boats cast off. Dawn was graying. "Let's go for a swim," said the professor.

Swims had become part of our routine, even at the expense of going to the Consulate. With the hope for visas at low ebb, we quit our regular routines and let the tides of the Mediterranean cool off body and soul. If we still strolled over to Montredon two or three times a week, it was almost more to see who else might be there than to keep bothering the doorman and the staff.

Frank and Mehring usually stayed in the bistro. While we three others were swimming, they sat in opposite corners, composing poetry or prose or writing letters, mostly to Switzerland. Mehring had his publisher there, and Frank a wealthy friend—the heroine of his *A Long Life with You*—who would send him money when he asked her for it.

Carli acted as postman and scout. His precious army discharge made it quite safe for him to take the streetcar to the city, mail our letters, and nose around for news or opportunities on the escape front. He would trot off with a sad face and a few longing glances back at Gumbel and me in the ocean. The beach was in sight of the road, and we hardly ever dared to sunbathe on it, but in the sea we felt safe. The athletic scholar would race me out and beat me diving through the breakers; though once upon a time, as a teenager, I had set records, he mostly stayed ahead. We would do the crawl until we were far out and drift farther, on and on. Somewhere ahead of us lay the coast of North Africa and the alleged destinations of the ships one heard whispers about: Algiers, Dakar, Casablanca.

Returning to the Bar Mistral one high noon, we found Carli back all excited. He had news, concrete news. One could buy visas to countries overseas—not to go there, but just to get the transit visas. The Portuguese would accept these overseas visas, and they were not even expensive: one to

China or the Belgian Congo cost only a hundred francs or so. They could be entered properly and legally, without any waiting, in any valid passport.

That left us out. "Carli," I said—nothing more. Gumbel's eyes lit up, though: Did this practice apply to French passports? Carli had no idea.

"Come on," said the professor. "Let's go exploring."

The streetcar ride downtown took less than half an hour. Carli did not want me along; he never did on these trips to the consulate quarter, where you could not always lose yourself in the crowd, as you could on the Cannebière. He said the *flics* were out in mass today, but I was simply too curious to stay behind. He was promptly proved right; we no sooner got off the streetcar than a police patrol headed for us. We looked around for Gumbel, but he had vanished.

Carli held out his document. The first policeman nodded. "*Et mademoiselle?*"

"*Ma fiancée,*" Carli replied.

"*Les papiers—*"

I rummaged through my pocketbook and gave the enemy a friendly smile along with my old *permis de séjour*. In this diversionary smile I had a lot of practice. And indeed, the long-past expiration date of the permit seemed to escape his notice. Something else puzzled him. "Not released from camp?"

"I never was in camp," I said with a shrug.

It surprised him. "*Comment?*"

I shrugged again.

He said, "*Ah, ça. . . .*"

Those two syllables always meant an impasse, a kind of mental short circuit. The uniformed ones looked at me. They must think I have Nazi connections, it flashed through my mind, or else I'd have been sent to Gurs like the rest, who had now found that women's camp in the Pyrenees their salvation. Before I knew what was happening, the obsolete permit was back in my hand. We were waved on.

For us, passportless, visa-shopping was pointless, but we thought it wiser to walk a few blocks down the street and not to take the trolley back while the *flics* might still have us in sight. The line at the Portuguese Consulate seemed even longer than usual. We were approaching it from the rear, and at the very end I was shocked to see the unmistakable figures of Franz and Alma Werfel. I saw the heavy man mopping his brow as the hot sun of the Midi burned down unmercifully. I knew he had a heart condition.

"Alma—Alma," I cried, running up to her, "how can you stand around like this, in this heat? You'll be waiting for hours!"

It was not so easy to bend Alma Mahler Werfel's iron will. "We need the visa," she said simply. "Franzl will have to endure it."

"But I can't imagine that they wouldn't let you in," I said, looking up and down the long line. Had Werfel's fame not spread in every language?

He was breathing heavily, trying to muster a brave smile. His face was ashen. "We wanted to send in our card," Alma explained, "but nothing gets past the doorman. We'll just have to wait."

I had an idea. "We won't be a minute," I promised, starting across the street with Carli on my heels. We ran to the corner café, found the telephone, looked up a number, made the call.

"*Consulat de Portugal,*" a brisk female voice answered.

"This is Madame Werfel speaking," I began. "You know— Franz Werfel, the writer?" I imitated Alma's French speech, her slight Viennese accent.

"*Oui, madame.*"

The brisk voice rang the least bit hesitant. It emboldened me. "May I talk to the consul, please?"

"One moment, Madame Werfel—"

In one moment the consul was on the line, telling me how much he admired my husband. When I had briefly explained the situation, he asked us to come to see him at four.

Swelling with pride, I returned to the Werfels. The line had not moved an inch. Werfel was leaning on Alma. "Come," I called happily, from far away; leading them out of the line, I told them of the appointment. Then—because Alma would have to know, after all—I added somewhat uncertainly that I had made the call as "Madame Werfel."

She embraced me. We joined Carli at the café, and at a corner table in the shade Alma declared, "Let's celebrate. ... *Garçon! une bouteille de champagne!*"

The color was slowly returning to Werfel's cheeks. "Thank you so much," he said to me. "Is there anything I could do for you?"

For me, I told him, it would not even make sense to stand in line for the Portuguese visa I needed. I had no passport.

"The Czech consul here is a friend of mine," he said after only a moment's thought. "I'll see if he can give you a Czech passport."

I could not thank him enough. I said my father came from Prague—perhaps that would help—and added quickly that Carli's birthplace was also in Czechoslovakia. Werfel promised to put in a word for both of us. Alma kept silent.

Next morning, however, she told me that the Portuguese consul had been charming; they had exchanged autographs with him, and now the Spanish one had given them an appointment by phone, with no trouble. As for us, we were expected at the Czech Consulate. . . . Yes, today. . . . Yes, Carli and I both.

The Czech Consulate in Marseilles was unique. Amidst surrender and appeasement, this anachronism continued its representation of an anti-Hitler government in exile. Its existence was akin to ours—here today, presumably in flight tomorrow—but the consul gave meaning to it. With a bold front he kept up bolder activities. In this overcrowded little Consulate the word, for once, was not "Red tape as usual, and the devil take the hindmost." It was "Save whom you can."

Carli and I went into a small room with half-emptied shelves, half-filled packing cases, and open file cabinets; there were all the signs of imminent dissolution and moving out, and yet there was time to help us. It turned out that this room in enemy country was a last bit of home ground. All at once we were together again, the Czechs and us. Twenty-two years had passed since they had broken free from the old monarchy on the Danube, but our common roots were still there, still valid, if only for passports for us.

At a window we were given application blanks, forms still received from London with the official seal of the Czechoslovak government of Eduard Beneš and Jan Masaryk. "We're using them while they last," said the girl who helped us fill them out—in French, for neither Carli nor I understood the Czech language.

At first we did not understand much of anything that went on, but within minutes the Czech girl was back with two passports. We could not believe our eyes as we thumbed through them and saw the official stamps, the photos we had brought, the dates we had given, and our names, mine with the Czech ending for women's names, "-ova." The only difference between these and regular Czechoslovak passports was the color of the jacket: Our brand-new ones were pink, not brown. One could see at a glance that they were something special.

We gave thanks and asked no questions, but before calling the next in line, the young woman volunteered a bit of information. "These passports have been helpful to many people," she said encouragingly. "Good luck to you—and give the consul's regards to Monsieur Werfel. . . . Tell him to send us more friends," she added under her breath.

We found the Werfels at the café where they used to have lunch. Mehring, too, had shown up; curiosity had got the better of his apprehensions. Our pink passports went from hand to hand, and everyone admired the consul's courage.

"Could you try sending me to him?" asked Mehring. "After all, Berlin isn't far from Prague. . . ."

Werfel gave him a note of introduction. It proved unnecessary. The consul knew Mehring's writings and gave him a passport at once—in another name, since Mehring feared to travel under his own. No lost platoon could try harder to make its remaining ammunition count than the Czechs in Marseilles as they hurried to use up their lifesaving pink papers.

From consulate to consulate we trotted, Mehring, Carli, and I, for Mehring was too arrest-prone to be left alone. Our next stop was the Chinese Consulate, the only one in Marseilles that would still sell overseas visas—the Belgian Congo had just gone off the market. Ironically, the only emigrés overseas one had never envied were the few in China. They also had been caught in a war, with the Japanese; almost all we knew about it was that the Nazis called the Japanese the Aryans of the East, but that sufficed. Perhaps it was as well that, as Mehring put it, our passports, those bits of pure fiction, would take only fictitious visas.

At the Chinese Consulate two friendly little men received us with enigmatic smiles. One vanished with our passports; the other asked in singingly accented French for a reference in China. Mehring did not have to think one up: An old acquaintance, the journalist Willy Haas, had joined the little exile colony in Shanghai in the early thirties. Our destination in China? Shanghai, of course. "One hundred francs each, please."

The three bills were hardly on the table when the other little man brought back the passports, adorned meanwhile with lovely vertically scribbled hieroglyphics. We bowed politely, departed with our embellished documents, and strolled as innocently as possible to the streetcar stop for Pointe Rouge. There was no more hurry; the Portuguese and Spanish Consulates had closed for the day, and a detailed inspection of the Chinese visas could await the safety of my little room. They looked like delightful ornaments, as decorative as they were mysterious.

"I can read mine perfectly," said Mehring. "It says: 'Entrance into China forbidden on pain of death' "—a translation that was soon repeated all over Marseilles by other carriers of these beautiful, unfathomable visas.

The joking did not last, of course. When Leonhard Frank said that he did not want a Chinese visa nor a Czech passport, for that matter—such things meant asking for trouble—Mehring caught the jitters about our "false papers." It did not help that Carli, after a day spent in line, brought them back with three perfectly good Portuguese transit visas. "You will never get through Spain with these things," Mehring prophesied.

That evening, gathered in my room as usual, we were frightened by a knock on the door. No one moved until the landlady's voice called my name. "A visitor for you."

Hesitantly, I opened the door. "*Un monsieur.*" She grinned. "He's waiting downstairs."

Carli followed me down, as for protection; the others stayed and shut the door. A gay, familiar laugh rang out in the bar, full of fishermen at that hour. . . . "*Chérie,*" Gilbert called, glass in hand already.

I found no words. He warmly greeted Carli; he had news for both of us—good news, of course—and for me a package from his younger sister. She was sending me some things to wear, very nice things, Gilbert said, which I could certainly use.

I opened the letter he handed me: a farewell note from Passer, written before embarking for England with other Czech officers. There was money in it too—my old publisher and friend could not know how providentially it came, with Carli's army pay all but used up—and a dry, oddly touching first sentence: "I hope this finds you alive."

183

Some discharged Czech soldiers had delivered the note to Gilbert on their way to Agen. He had wanted to bring it to me in person. Then he took my hand. "*Chérie*, I'll take you home with me."

Home . . . of course, there was no home for me . . . but as he said it, the word rang altogether natural. The Bar Mistral seemed changed; all of a sudden it was as if we belonged in the cheerful circle of the natives. The new arrival obviously pleased the innkeeper's wife.

"A bottle of Bordeaux, madame," Gilbert ordered, leading Carli and me to a table in the corner. There we sat, the three of us, and I looked silently at Gilbert. Madame brought the wine and had an amiable nod for us while pouring. We clinked glasses, and Gilbert brought out his favorite toast: "*À nos amours. . . .*"

I had to get hold of myself. I had to remind myself that any dream of becoming a French peasant girl had burst a long time ago, at the gendarmerie. I smiled, feeling a little lost, and went on drinking and wondering. Did Gilbert not know the risks involved in hiding someone like me? It was I who did not know then that already in those days a French resistance movement had come into being in the region of Toulouse and that Gilbert, my pacifist who "wouldn't have gone into the army anyway," had been in it from the start.

Our third bottle was on the house. It came with the announcement that Madame just happened to have a room free for M. Dubois, and with an invitation from her husband to a day's fishing. Gilbert accepted with pleasure. "Fishing is our national sport," he used to say, "the best excuse for looking at the water and doing nothing."

We were both leaving at the same unearthly hour of dawn, Gilbert to go fishing with the men of Pointe Rouge and I to stand in line with Carli at the Spanish Consulate. The Spanish visa could not be obtained by one for all; each applicant had to make a personal appearance. To Mehring the reason seemed plain: "Because they'll keep our false passports and

184

turn us over to the Gestapo." Under the new circumstances he refused to join us but felt obliged as a friend to give me a solemn warning: "Your Frenchman is a spy, of course."

Did he really think so? I never found out. I did not really expect trouble with the Spanish visa. Still, a good deal of thought and preparation went into this last link in the paper chain that should keep us afloat if ever we got out of France—a big if, but useless to worry about. We could take only one step at a time. Carli carried only his pink passport. The *prestataire* discharge stayed in his room; what was good for French policemen would remind the Spaniards of his military age and suggest that he might go on fighting their Nazi friends elsewhere. As for me, I carefully did my hair and chose the most becoming dress from Gilbert's package; the flight had shown how important it could be to look your best in the worst situations. Fortunately Gilbert's pretty sister was my size.

"Good luck," said Mehring. Then, pulling his beret down in front as usual to look more French, he suddenly decided to come along after all. His suit was badly frayed; nobody had thought of bringing him a new one. Head down, he stood between us in the line outside the Consulate, still short so early in the morning. A cool breeze blew in from the sea and made me think enviously of Gumbel, who would be taking a swim now.

Before long the line moved us inside, to be greeted by a colossal portrait of Generalissimo Franco and a loud, clear "Mehring!" from a woman in line in front of us. Mehring frantically pressed his finger to his lips and shook his head— it was because of this place that he had changed his name on the Czech passport—but the woman came over anyway. Without hesitation Carli took her place in line. I covered Mehring.

I recognized her now: She was our colleague Adrienne Thomas, the author of a pacifist novel that had been a best-seller after World War I. "Here everything goes like clockwork," she said confidently, "if you have an exit visa, of course." Alsatian-born, she proudly clutched her French passport.

"But we can't get one!" My voice, raised in anger, made her retreat hastily. I looked back for Mehring; behind me stood a tall stranger. Carli, advanced almost to the desk, was waving to me; I managed to squeeze in next to him and whisper in his ear: "Walter's gone. . . ." He shrugged, handing the clerk our two passports.

Only Spanish was spoken here, not French; catching just a word now and then increased our discomfort. A gesture indicated that we should wait under the portrait of the generalissimo. Adrienne left with her visa, looking the other way. At last we were summoned again. Lo and behold, beside the Chinese drawing and the Portuguese stamp in each pink passport was a Spanish transit visa.

Outside, back in the fresh air, we each took a deep breath. But where was Mehring? We looked in the café where we used to meet the Werfels; their corner table was vacant. He would not dare run about Marseilles alone, we thought. We hoped to find him back at Pointe Rouge, but only Leonhard Frank and Gilbert were there, conversing animatedly in sign language over a basket of fresh fish. A fine catch, Gilbert said; he would personally make a pot of bouillabaisse for us. I knew his cooking was first-rate.

"Mehring has disappeared," I told him, and Carli translated for Frank.

Frank registered no surprise. "Wherever he goes, a hand will reach down from heaven to arrest Mehring," he said and announced his customary departure for the American Consulate.

"I'll look for him," said Carli.

"Where?" I wanted to come too.

"You'd better go to the Consulate," Carli decided. "Maybe he's there."

Gilbert, always agreeable to everything, advised us only to be back in two hours, when the bouillabaisse would be ready.

Far ahead Leonhard Frank was striding down the beach. "Let me ask at the police station," said Carli.

"Please don't," I said. "Police can only do harm."

We caught Frank in the park. Ahead of us were the white steps, the doorman at the portal, the usual beggar groups. Before I could look around, Frank took my arm and drew me up the steps; he always liked to have an interpreter with him in case of need. Carli stayed outside to look under the trees. He had never been to the Consulate; his case was not yet pending.

Inside it was so crowded that I could not see the secretary, nor she me. To me, coming in out of the sun, it seemed almost dark; the reception room seemed full of waiting shadows. One small, delicate one now detached itself from the twilight to approach me, head ducked, a beret in clenched fingers. . . . "Walter," I stammered.

"They nabbed me on the Cannebière," he whispered, still out of breath. "I was running too fast from the Spanish Consulate—they were going to chain me——"

"Walter! No fictions, please."

He caught his breath. "First they wanted to know just who I am—and at the station house—before the inspector came—I managed to flush the false papers down the toilet——"

"The passport, Walter? The precious visas?" I wrung my hands.

He nodded. "They searched me later—all naked——"

"Walter!"

"Half naked." He corrected himself. "But if they had found the papers on me. . . ." He kept close to me as we headed for the door. "When they let me go, I came here to the Americans—I couldn't think of any other place, with your spy at the bistro. . . ."

187

Through a gap in the waiting crowd I suddenly saw the girl at the desk. She was looking at me. "Madame Pauli," she said quite clearly. *"Monsieur le consul vous attend."*

That was impossible. . . . My knees shook more than they had during the bombings; I had to hold on to Mehring. Then I made my way to the desk.

"The consul is expecting you," the American girl repeated. Instead of going somewhere, I had to sit down. What could have happened? The room was still turning when the girl got up and led me to the holy of holies.

Good that I have a decent dress on, it ran through my mind as a gentleman behind a large, clean desk rose to offer me a chair. Then I sat facing him. He took up a piece of paper. "Miss Pauli, your visa has arrived."

I could only shake my head. It seemed unbelievable. There was some more—something about its being only a visitor's visa, granted as an exception, a rescue visa—and then I was handed a printed sheet. "Because you have no passport," the gentleman said. "For stateless persons."

It had to be me: There, at the top, was my name. . . . "Fill out the blanks, and bring the signed form back here," said Mr. Bingham. I was dismissed.

Waiting outside were Mehring and Frank. "Has the answer come?" they asked in unison.

"I don't know," I said. "A visa—for me!"

Walter fell silent. "No," Frank exclaimed, "that can't be! You cannot get an American visa before me—I'm much better known."

That was a fact. I realized only later that in America women are saved first. At the time the great Leonhard Frank was furious; whether he ever forgave me, I do not know.

"Take me along," said Walter. How I would have loved to. . . .

And Carli said, "Herthalein, I'm so glad," with tears in his eyes.

Frank stayed at the Consulate—to lodge a complaint, I suppose. The three of us set out for the bouillabaisse. The miracle paper, two folded sheets, lay in my handbag.

At the Bar Mistral we were greeted by Gilbert and the delicious aroma of his bouillabaisse. "All set," he called, beaming.

"I got my American visa," I said tonelessly.

The merest shadow crossed Gilbert's brow; a moment later he was laughing again. "You can't leave here, can you?"

For a moment we had forgotten.

CHAPTER 10

Manhunt

Without the help of a man named Varian Fry, all of us would nevertheless have gone under in Marseilles, and thousands with us. In New York, a quarter of a century after his rescue operation, Fry was decorated with the Croix du Chevalier of the French Legion of Honor and extolled as "America's greatest undercover agent" of World War II.

In August, 1940, when Fry showed up in Marseilles, our prospects of getting out looked dimmer than ever. Though I had not realized it at first, even recipients of the U.S. visas that arrived in driblets were really being mocked by fate. An admission ticket to the Promised Land made it only more unbearable to know that the road remained closed. We were still in a mousetrap with no exit.

With the American paper in your hands you had no business anymore at the castle in Montredon. The consulate could and would not mix in the internal affairs of other countries. You were free to enter the United States. How? That was your worry.

Where there is a visa, there must be a way, I thought, and in a burst of courage I ventured right into the lions' den of the Police Prefecture. Perhaps, having come by a miracle, the American document would work another miracle and get me a legal exit visa. Gilbert, deeply distrustful of the police of his country, insisted on coming along. "Hold onto your paper," he warned me. "Don't let them touch it. *Il faut se méfier.*"

He accompanied me only as an escort; Frenchmen of military age never got permission to leave, for fear they might join De Gaulle's "Free French" in England. Besides—which I still did not know then—Gilbert was already in the resistance movement that was just beginning. "They can't bother us here," he had assured me when the Nazis swallowed other countries; when it became clear that Clairac might be bothered, everything changed, but he did not tell me that. "If I can't get out," he told me, "I'll wait for you here till the war is over."

The official at the Prefecture hardly glanced at my American paper. He had only to hear the words "exit visa" to spread his hands: "*Ah, ça. . . .*" This matter was beyond the competence of local authorities; exit permits for foreigners were issued only in Vichy. Applications had to be made there, in person.

In Vichy? The capital of Marshal Pétain, who had signed the French capitulation? Apply in person to Hitler's collaborators, who in the infamous Article 19 of the Armistice had promised to "surrender on demand" all persons claimed as "Germans" by the "German Government in France"? God preserve us from Vichy, I thought as we left the Prefecture.

"First they wouldn't let us in; now they won't let us out," I said, storming at Gilbert.

Que faire? "You can travel with this as with a passport,"

the consul had said when he handed me the American paper. Precisely that put me into a new dilemma, for travel to America—supposing I managed to make my way out of France—required Spanish and Portuguese transit visas, and those I already had in my "false" Czech passport, which was not acceptable to American authorities. Two kinds of papers seemed as bad as none. I couldn't risk another visit to the Spaniards. They kept records, not just for themselves but also for their sinister backers who rode through the streets of Marseilles in black limousines, wearing long gray overcoats, high black boots, and peaked caps on which the swastika glittered.

Gilbert knew where comfort was possible and where it was not. "Don't worry," he said. "If you get out, I'll wait for you."

If. . . . Desperate stories mingling rumor and fact were told about attempts to escape illegally. It was a rumor that anyone caught trying to cross the frontier without a permit would be handed over to the Gestapo; it was a fact that one such, the art critic Karl Einstein, an authority on African sculpture, had simply been sent back to Marseilles and had hanged himself there—nobody knew why. And it was a fact that ship's passages were being sold on the black market; but did the ships exist, or were they just rumors?

The black limousines were not; they had been sighted in town and in the suburbs. The only unoccupied border seemed to be the park at Montredon, where the human tide around the marble steps kept rising. For each visa that arrived inside, ten new beggars joined the wait under the beeches that gave some relief from the heat. And quite often it was for the dead, not for the living, that Washington sent visas. The forms for Ernst Weiss, the novelist who had committed suicide when the Germans entered Paris, for Walter Hasenclever, the playwright who had killed himself in an internment camp—those forms came and lay there and remained blank.

Suddenly, out of nowhere, a new rumor spread from the heart of Marseilles to the crowds around the Consulate and to Pointe Rouge, where our little group was hiding in the Bar Mistral. Help was coming, one person whispered to another: Somebody was due from across the ocean, an American, a messenger, an envoy, an ambassador? Everyone knew something; no one knew anything. From the Bar Mistral Carli still went to town daily, and when I could not stand the waiting, I went along. The little cafés too were hideouts; refugees spent days and nights there, sticking together, taking fright when any stranger entered.

"Be careful," our colleague Hans Natonek warned in a low voice. "A fellow here claims to know the name of an American he says is looking for us. Wants only fifty francs. But when you've paid, he asks for your name and address."

The American appeared to be a trap. Reach for it, and the lid fell shut and cut your head off, perhaps. Nervously we moved on, from café to café, looking around and behind us—were we being followed by agents in high black boots?

The Werfels sat in their accustomed place. We greeted them, and when I ventured a question about the rumors, Alma put a finger to her lips. "Ssh—let's not talk about that. Franzl gets too excited."

"The American?" Franz Werfel's lips were white. "He's supposed to be in Vichy—they're trying to trap us——"

"Don't excite yourself, Franzl," Alma pleaded, motioning for us to go away.

Back at the Bar Mistral we found Mehring with Leonhard Frank. The poet and the novelist were studying a paper in Frank's hand. "Your visa?" I asked hopefully. Now, perhaps, I'd be forgiven for getting mine ahead of Frank's, despite his fame. . . .

It was not his visa. It was a cable received for him at the Consulate; no, not Thomas Mann's reply either—not directly, at least. It came from Hermann Kesten, our lucky, witty literary friend who had escaped from Paris in time and had gone to New York. The text now pondered by the two German men of letters was in French so as not to be held up by the censor: "VISA DE SECOURS SUIVANT PAR MESSAGER PEU-TETRE"—"Rescue visa following by messenger maybe."

Mehring hunched his shoulders. "They just say that so we won't kill ourselves too."

Frank stared glumly at the sheet. " '*Messager*' means 'messenger'; I know that. But what is '*peutetre*'?"

Mehring jumped up. "I told you," he cried. " '*Peut-être*' means 'maybe'—'perhaps'—'maybe yes, maybe no,' " he said, pacing up and down as if in a cage.

Frank's piercing eyes followed him. "Of course. But does it mean more 'yes' or more 'no'?"

Mehring stopped abruptly. "It means 'maybe.' "

And Frank stubbornly kept at it: " 'Maybe yes' or 'maybe no'?"

They never settled the question. Frank raised it over and over, on every possible and impossible occasion, until the word sprouted wings for us, hung in the air, and spun about our heads—about life and death, maybe. . . .

Like rats on a sinking ship, we huddled in groups all that August, hiding all over Marseilles. There was no way even to desert the ship. We were doomed to sink with it.

When rats are jammed into too small a hole, they start eating each other. We did not do that, but we began not to trust one another. Everyone seemed to harbor some secret he would not share. Sometimes you thought you had picked up a clue, had heard the American rescuer's name mentioned in some hushed conversation, for instance; when you asked about it, the reply was a shrug. The seas kept rising all around us; whenever a lifeboat showed on the horizon, everyone wanted to be the first to get in—and then the lifeboat would fade away in the mist.

The days grew shorter; the nights seemed endless. A week felt like a year. And after all, when you looked at it soberly, what was there to expect? "I can't stay any longer," Gilbert said late in the month. His parents could not run the shop by themselves; they needed him. "But I'll soon be back with you. We'll see each other again, *chérie.*"

We parted at a street corner. We did not see each other again—everything happened so fast then—and at bottom I was not really counting on it when he waved to me for the last time. I stood looking after him, never turning my head, though he was long out of sight. Then finally I walked on, without thinking, without knowing where. Suddenly I found myself down by the Vieux Port.

I thought I heard the lobsters screaming, but it was only the fishwives hawking their wares. I fled, blindly, almost colliding with a myopic pedestrian who had not seen me either. "Hertha," she exclaimed when the collision had been averted by a hair, "how good to run into you!" I recognized a colleague from Vienna.

She is a journalist and what the French call a *débrouillard*, a survival artist. Blond, chubby all around, and always radiating cheer, she has a knack for somehow getting through the worst situations; in those days it was a talent beyond price. She and I had first met at my literary agency in Vienna and then at Parisian refugee aid committees, where I came to appreciate her skill at getting money for herself and others and dispensing good advice. The next time our paths crossed, in Marseilles, she had just come directly from Gurs, the women's internment camp, and she was proud of it. "Wasn't I smarter than you?" she demanded. "I didn't have to dodge bombs with Mehring."

So she had already gleaned this tidbit. She knew everything. She could hear the grass grow and could see through stone walls from behind her thick lenses. The tales of the many times this ability had put her back on her feet were narrated as lovingly as the romances of our famous colleagues, which she would garnish with details of her own.

I used to be skeptical about her own conquests until years

later, in America, I witnessed one. With my own eyes I saw her wooed by a handsome man who owned vineyards in the Hudson Valley. He went so far as to crawl through her bedroom window at night—only to be promptly and indignantly ejected.

In 1940, walking with me between the fishwives of the Vieux Port, her arm in mine, she murmured furtively that she had something to tell me. I scarcely listened. Now I'll hear all about her latest affair, it ran through my mind. And she confided, "He's staying at the Splendide."

An expectant pause. "Who is he?" I asked, just to be polite.

She basked a moment in my ignorance before enlightening me under her breath: "The American, of course."

I stood speechless.

"I've been turned away already; I'm not on his list. But perhaps you are, and he'll see you." Her important mien dissolved into one great smile. "Well," she said, beaming, "am I a friend or not? Go to it. And let me know." Before I could thank her, she disappeared among the fishwives.

The Hôtel Splendide was only a few blocks away, at the corner of the Cannebière and the Boulevard d'Athènes. To my surprise I found the lobby deserted; only two policemen were standing around, following me with their eyes as I approached the desk to ask for—whom? Too late I realized that I had forgotten to get the American's name.

I stammered something about an American gentleman. It must have sounded right, or familiar, at least, for the desk clerk nodded. "No unannounced admittance," he declared.

I whispered my name. When he shouted it over the house telephone, I thought I could hear the steps of the *flics* at my back, coming to make the arrest. The clerk put down the receiver. "Fourth floor, please," he said as if it were a matter of course. "Last room to the left."

I barely reached the elevator. The tight little box rose

with me, choking off my breath; any moment, I knew, we'd be stuck . . . but the cage opened. Fourth floor. I turned left. A dark hallway led to a sliver of light, an open door. The sea breeze blew from a window high above the Vieux Port, and the window framed a picture in the blue haze: the silhouette of Notre Dame de la Garde. Otherwise the walls of the room were bare.

A young man sitting in shirt sleeves at an empty table ignored me for a few moments, his attention focused on a piece of paper. I waited, embarrassed. Was I in the right place? Absentmindedly the young man raised his head, and his eyes brushed over me through horn-rimmed glasses.

"Well, Miss Pauli," said a dry voice, "I've got you on my list." It seemed not to surprise him at all. Not a muscle twitched in his expressionless face. It was what I called a Buster Keaton face, and learning to see through it would take time.

That his name was Varian Fry was all I learned about him at that first encounter. The conversation was brief and matter-of-fact; what our rescuer-to-be called his usual first interview proceeded somewhat as if I were applying for a job. I did not have to struggle through more than three or four sentences of broken English before he switched to French for the rest of the interrogation. His French was fluent, with hardly a trace of an accent.

My answers seemed to satisfy him for the moment. He had been looking for me, he said, but in fact I had happened to come at a good time; yesterday all his visitors had been picked up in the lobby and removed by the police in paddy wagons.

I gave a start, which he seemed not to notice; he talked on calmly, without a break, without a change in his voice. The whole lot had been quickly released, he said, thanks to the cordial relations he had established with an inspector of the Sûreté. Then, of course, it had been necessary to destroy all evidence in this room, in case a search was made of it— because, as I probably knew, the Gestapo might take a hand in it. He was down to a basic list of names again, he said.

He showed me the paper. My name caught my eye, between "Hans Natonek, Czech humorist" and "Ernst Weiss, Czech novelist." With Natonek he was in touch, said Fry. What did I know about Weiss? I told him. He took a pencil, turned the list around, and crossed Weiss off. The pencil wandered to two previous deletions. "Einstein . . . Hasenclever . . . now I have three vacancies," said Varian Fry.

I understood: It was a matter of vacancies. They silenced us. Dead men do not talk, and neither did we, the living. People in our situation must protect their vacancies.

Following the crossed-out Weiss on the list was "Walter Mehring, German poet," and there I had better news to give. "Bar Mistral," Fry jotted down in the margin. Then the Buster Keaton face turned to me: "Bring Mehring with you tomorrow. *Au revoir.*"

Somehow I got back to our beach hideout. The rumor had taken shape: It was an average American, tall, young, bespectacled, named Varian Fry. We no longer needed to hunt for our man; he was hunting for us. Tomorrow I was to bring Mehring.

I gave Walter the message, but he was full of suspicions. Who was behind this American? Where did he come from? What would he do with us? "Ask him," was all I could say.

Hesitantly, the beret pulled deep over his eyes, Walter came as far as the streetcar stop in the morning, but when a black Mercedes rounded the corner ahead, he was gone. I went on alone. In the city I decided to look for the Werfels first; if they knew, I wanted their opinion, and if they had not heard about it yet, I meant to tell them that the American was not in Vichy but at the Splendide.

As usual, they knew more than I did. "We had dinner with Mr. Fry last night," said Alma, signaling the waiter to bring an aperitif to their table for me. "A nice young man, but I don't know whether to trust him."

She gave a vivid account of the dinner and of the cordials afterwards; of herself pleading every time they clinked glasses, "You must save us, Mr. Fry!" while he sat with his unmoved stone face; and finally of her murmured warning to Franzl to be on his guard and of Fry's interruption—"Excuse me, Frau Werfel, but I understand some German"—delivered in perfect German, without cracking a smile. And all that he claimed to have in mind for us was a ship, a project like the ones used to fleece us on the black market, although Mr. Fry hadn't asked for money yet. We just had to wait and see what came of the imaginary ship, sighed Alma.

Alone or not, I wanted to find out more. This time a line of people I did not know was waiting in the lobby of the Splendide, and when I was finally summoned to the fourth floor, the last room to the left had changed completely. It looked like a regular office now, with a secretary clicking away on a new typewriter, and in Fry's stead another young man came toward me, locked the door, and introduced himself: "I'm Beamish." I later found that this was Fry's nickname for the German refugee whose discharge papers from the French Army identified him as "Albert Hermant." Today Albert Hirschmann—his real name—teaches at Harvard, then Fry's recent alma mater.

"This is Lena," said Beamish, nodding toward the typist. She looked familiar, and it turned out that I had seen her before: Until Paris fell, Polish-born Lena Fishman had worked there for a refugee relief committee. She and Beamish formed the nucleus of what Fry called his "underground outfit." Fry himself was sprawling on the bed amid a profusion of papers and dictating to Lena—dictating letters to protégés whose addresses he had obtained.

"Where is Mehring?" was how he greeted me, not looking up.

I confessed the truth: Mehring had been scared off by a Mercedes.

Fry interrupted his dictation. "What do you say, Lena?"

"*Il ne faut pas exagérer*," said Lena calmly. "Let's not exaggerate" was her favorite bit of advice and helped in most cases. She offered to come with me to fetch Mehring, and when Fry approved the idea, she drew compact and lipstick from her pocketbook and announced, *"Je fais ma petite beauté"*—an invariable ritual whenever she went out.

Aware of the importance of looking my best for all eventualities, I also used the mirror in Fry's closet for a quick repair job. Behind this mirror was a hiding place for maps and other dangerous documents, I heard later.

She knew Walter Mehring from Paris, Lena told me on our way. *"Mais je n'ai pas couché avec,"* she added merrily, and this unusual statement startled me only the first time, until I heard her repeat it about other gentlemen. It was another of Lena's pet sayings that served to cheer people up.

We found Walter alone, and she set out to dispel his misgivings. Fry, she explained, had been sent over by the Emergency Rescue Committee, a private organization in New York, with no other aim than to save as many as possible of the writers, artists, intellectuals, who were trapped in France and in danger of their lives. Our cry for help to Thomas Mann had arrived together with the news of the fall of Paris, which stirred a wave of concern.

When word came of the "surrender on demand" clause in the Armistice, the committee swung into action. Its efforts and the intercession of Eleanor Roosevelt led the President to authorize the "special emergency rescue visas" that would enable us to enter the United States as visitors, even though we could not return home. For all that, however, we were still trapped in France.

Fry was here to get us out. He had arrived with his pockets full of lists bearing over two hundred names and only a handful of addresses; at first he had thought he might have to bicycle around unoccupied France, looking for people on his lists. He knew a number of names on them: writers such as Werfel and Heinrich Mann, painters such as Marc Chagall and Max Ernst, sculptors like Jacques Lipchitz, musicians like Wanda Landowska. Most of the names he had never heard of; but known or unknown, he was trying now to find, to aid, to save, them all, to get them out from "under the noses of the Gestapo," as he liked to put it.

"By ship?" I asked.

Lena shrugged. *"Une idée comme une autre.* He'll use it if it works. There are other ways."

"So now we are on two lists," Walter Mehring summed up; "one for delivery to death, the other for deliverance to life— maybe. . . ."

Lena powdered her face. *"Il ne faut pas exagérer,"* she said. "Come along."

"Mehring is one of the best German poets," Fry reported after that first encounter, "but so small that we called him Baby. In the dirty, unpressed clothes he was wearing when he got to Marseilles he looked more like a tramp than a poet— or a baby." Yet the name stuck. To Fry and his "underground outfit," Walter remained "Baby." They had such names for everyone they frequently discussed—it eliminated the risk of a police spy or German agent overhearing a name he knew from a "wanted" list—and Mehring was one they had to discuss very frequently. "Things went all right till Mehring came," Fry used to say. "With him, trouble started."

The rescue ship was still a mirage then, but chances for escape overland, through Spain, were improving. When you listened to Fry, it really seemed a breeze. If possible, he assured us, the border police would look the other way. "If you hit the right man, he'll let you through; if you run into the wrong one, you're sent back. It's a matter of luck," he said.

In fact, of course, he did not want us to depend on luck alone. The whole frontier zone, where the foothills of the Pyrenees meet the Mediterranean, was carefully reconnoitered. Contacts with French resistance groups were established, and through them with Spanish anti-Fascists, to learn how to avoid French border guards and which of the Spanish could and could not be trusted. The route and routine of every patrol for thirty miles inland was studied. An identification system was worked out: Each refugee leaving Marseilles was given half of a torn card with a number on it; the other half, bearing the same number, was held by the liaison man on the frontier who would direct him across and tell him where to go and how to find "the right man." This was how Fry built his "underground railroad."

In the end it was a matter of luck after all. Some simply took a train and rode across the border, even without exit visas; the great majority had to walk over the hills. People with false papers might be arrested, they might be sent back, or they might be passed or even shown the way. This last sometimes happened precisely when they admitted that the papers were false. It came down to luck—and Mehring was the first whose luck ran out.

By then he had received his visa from the consulate—on a travel document like mine, officially termed "affidavit in lieu of passport"—and a torn numbered card to identify him to one of Fry's most reliable contacts in the border zone. He never got there. In Perpignan, where he had an hour's wait between trains, he was nabbed while sitting innocently at a café, relieved to have come that far without trouble.

When Fry heard the story, he had only one explanation: Baby's appearance must have convinced local detectives that at last they had some hobo wanted for six months of petty crime. Once under arrest, Walter landed in the police headquarters, where he was found to be a foreigner traveling without the necessary "safe conduct." In consequence of this discovery he was handcuffed and taken to the nearby concentration camp of St. Cyprien. He managed to send word to Fry, who hired a lawyer; no one ever knew how it came about, but one day Fry's Baby was returned to him at the Splendide, still wearing handcuffs.

Mehring dared not venture into the street again, not even to renew his old *permis de séjour*, which had expired in the meantime. Fry put him up at the Splendide and got a doctor to certify that M. Mehring was a sick man, confined to bed, and not expected to be up for weeks. Thus it happened that long after Carli and I were over the hills, Walter remained Fry's most present and persistent worry. Every knock on the door made the "patient" dive into bed—fully dressed, for instance, with his shoes sticking out from under the coverlet.

"If we find anything suspicious around you," Fry had been warned by his friendly police inspector, "we'll have to arrest you too. It's out of our hands. *Vous comprenez?*" Everyone understood. Fry assured the inspector that he was engaged in strictly legal activities: helping refugees get their visas, providing financial assistance, and so forth. To stress the point he moved his outfit to a small office near the hotel and christened it American Relief Center. The staff was growing: Miriam Davenport, an art student from Smith College and, like Lena, a Parisian acquaintance of Mehring's, became office manager and receptionist; the third in command, after Fry and Beamish, was now a young Austrian we knew, "Franzi" von Hildebrand, son of a celebrated theologian who was then hiding in Marseilles and was high on Fry's list. On and off, about a dozen people worked at the Centre Américain de Secours.

Fry made sure that appearances were maintained. The working day began at 8 A.M., when the first refugees were admitted, and was passed in interviewing them, registering data on cards, and filing the information. The last clients often left after midnight. Then, behind locked doors, the real work began: the staff conference at which the cases of the day were discussed and plans laid for their handling. The main points were always three: Whom to add to the list? What papers were needed? How would the flight take place?

The very first point caused a racking of brains. The question was delicate. One invariable rule was never to aid people who were not known to someone Fry could trust—he would take no chance on informers traveling his escape routes. In literary cases Mehring knew either the people themselves or all about them; in others, Franzi's connection with Catholic refugee groups helped. Besides, what Fry called the conspiracy at the Splendide extended from the fourth floor down to the third, to the room of Frank Bohn, a former German Social Democrat whom the American Federation of Labor had sent to Marseilles to help exiled European labor leaders. The two secret envoys were working closely together, and after Bohn's return to America Fry took over the responsibility for the remaining trade unionists, especially for the two in greatest danger, the two former German cabinet members named Breitscheid and Hilferding, who had previously been rumored missing.

The original two hundred names on Fry's list became two thousand; instead of the one month he had expected to spend in Marseilles, he spent thirteen, for Fry would yield only to force. He did not leave his post until he was arrested at the request of the Gestapo. Even then, French police had to escort him to the border to assure compliance with an expulsion order issued on the ground that he had "helped Jews and anti-Nazis."

To get his secret messages across the border Fry used what he called his toothpaste trick. First Lena typed the text on strips of thin paper; then these were rolled up tight, covered with a rubber finger, and slid into the bottom end of a half-emptied toothpaste tube. With the bottoms carefully closed again, these tubes looked like any others and were given to steady-nerved refugees with instructions to mail them to New York from Lisbon if all went well.

Upon arrival, the tubes were sifted by the New York committee, where Hermann Kesten did the work, not Thomas Mann. In Hollywood, where Mann lived now, a group of writers was getting film-script contracts for colleagues whose names would help the rescue effort: Mehring, Frank, Feuchtwanger, Heinrich Mann, Werfel, graced this list of the elect, on which Weiss and Hasenclever also appeared again, in vain. Added to it were Hans Lustig, who had movie experience, and our friend Friedrich Torberg, a young novelist freshly discharged from the Czech Army, in which he had served as a volunteer in Passer's battalion. From him we heard of Passer's safe landing on British soil some months before.

The British—whom Fry helped to get out hundreds of their own interned soldiers—were one of several sources from which he kept trying to get ships for those of his charges whom he could not risk sending through Spain; but instead of sailing, these "ghost ships," as Fry called them, used to evaporate into the Mediterranean mists. To estimate the urgency of his cases he managed to obtain copies of the weekly "wanted lists" of the Gestapo, and in assigning flight possibilities, he would follow these lists.

Among all the people on his own lists Fry found only one who did not consider himself in danger. Marc Chagall, the painter, had French papers; he was not only unpolitical but quite *"en règle"* and could not see why he should be on any list, including Fry's. Fry had a hard time even finding the master, who lived with his wife in the crumbling village of Gordes. He was busy painting cows and would not let the visitor disturb him. His work comes first, Fry thought, and withdrew.

One day, as the situation grew more critical, Chagall did show up at the Splendide. "Do you have beautiful cows in America?" was how he opened the conversation. Fry had to convince him that American cows were quite as good to paint as French ones before he would agree to leave.

The following morning Chagall's wife came back in despair. The police had come for her husband in the middle of the night, simply because he admitted being a Jew. She had been left free. What could be done?

Fry called the police inspector. "Do you know whom you arrested last night?"

"No idea."

"Monsieur Chagall," Fry explained, "is one of the world's most famous living artists. If this gets out, there'll be a scandal such as you've never seen. *Entendez, mon ami:* If Marc Chagall isn't free in half an hour, I'll give the story to *The New York Times* bureau in Vichy, and Vichy will be greatly embarrassed."

The ultimatum worked; in half an hour Chagall was at liberty, and Vichy even granted him an exit visa, then a great exception. "See you again in New York," Fry said to him in farewell, as he did to all of us. It always worked like a magic formula, he said. At the same time he would casually slip us our travel money. . . .

When the scant three thousand dollars he had brought along ran out, Fry found himself facing a new problem. The committee kept raising funds in America, but anything cabled openly to France would have to be accounted for to French authorities, which might make its use for underground work impossible. Then, in a restaurant called Seven Little Fishermen, Beamish discovered a pipeline. Jacques, the owner, who used to sit behind the cash register in seeming innocence, was reputedly the head of Marseilles's leading Corsican gang and up to his neck in white slavery, dope-smuggling, and the black market. It took some time before Jacques would let Beamish look behind the scenes because he knew Beamish was working for Fry, and Jacques disliked Americans. "They're not honest," he would say.

His suspicions once overcome, Jacques became most co-operative. He introduced Beamish to a Russian who called himself Dimitru and who knew people eager to get money out of France in a hurry, before it was too late. An agreement was reached: the Rescue Committee in New York would pay dollars to any lawyer or agent designated by Dimitru's clients, and Dimitru would pay the equivalent in francs to Fry's American Relief Center. "We worked together very well, we and the Corsican gangsters," Fry told us later, when we saw him again in New York.

In Marseilles he confined himself to casual observations. "Back home," he might say, "travel takes a wallet full of cash; here it takes a pocketful of papers." No amount of cash could help him get false papers for the most endangered though. Suddenly an idea came with the arrival of a young Viennese cartoonist, Bill Freier, whose unflattering portraits of the Führer had put him into a concentration camp. Fry had him purchase blank identity cards in the tobacco shops of Marseilles, fill them out as needed with names and dates, and then, with his brush, add the official rubber stamp of the prefecture. It looked quite genuine, especially after Fry gave it the final touch by throwing Freier's masterpieces on the floor and trampling on them in his socks until they looked worn and discovery-proof.

Freier got the equivalent of fifty cents per card, enough for him and Mina, his beloved girl friend, to live on; besides, Fry put the two of them on his list. They were later said to have perished, which was an error; actually they escaped. "The whole thing sounds too improbable to talk about," Fry said many years after it happened.

The impression Fry made on us was described meanwhile by our friend Hans Sahl, the poet and translator of poets. "You have to imagine: The borders were closed, you were trapped, any moment you could be arrested again, life was at an end—and suddenly standing there is a young American in his shirt sleeves who stuffs your pocket full of money, puts his arm around you in a poor imitation of a conspirator's manner, and whispers, 'Oh, there are ways to get you out; there are ways. . . .'"

Then Fry would pour the escapee a glass of whisky. "Besides, you need a new suit. You can't run around like this. Tomorrow we'll buy you a nice summer suit."

This was presumably the lesson Fry had learned in Mehring's case. Mehring, when my turn came to leave for the border, was still afraid to leave his hotel, though, so Fry presented me with another traveling companion, a young man whom I first took for a mountain guide. He looked the part, with his Tyrolean hat on his head and a pipe in his mouth, but he turned out to be a fellow writer, Norbert Muhlen. I knew him by name as the biographer of Dr. Hjalmar Schacht, Hitler's financial wizard.

Hans Natonek was scheduled to go with us; he wanted to take a young Czech blonde along, and Muhlen asked to bring his friend Hilde Walter. Hilde was a journalist from Berlin; until 1933 she had worked there for *Die Weltbuehne*, the famous magazine edited by Carl von Ossietzky, and in the midthirties she and Muhlen and Willy Brandt—then a refugee in Norway—had collaborated in the drive to win the Nobel Peace Prize for Ossietzky, then imprisoned in a Nazi concentration camp.

As for me, I did not want to leave without Carli, although he had no American visa and was not on Fry's list. I had an idea: Since Muhlen wasn't a mountain guide after all, perhaps Carli could serve in that role. I took him to the Splendide, and after a short interview Fry found him suitable. He went to his closet, produced a paper from behind the mirror, and spread it on the table.

It was a map. At the bottom it showed the town of Banyuls and a road behind its cemetery, running inland. At the top a line of crosses indicated the French-Spanish frontier, with arrows marking the French border posts that had to be avoided. Shown in between were various landmarks: a dry riverbed, vineyards, a Norman tower.

Carli carefully copied the map. He still has it. We were to take it along and to correct it where necessary, and once we had the right Spanish crossing point in sight, Carli was to turn back and to guide another group, while I continued with the first one.

Fry explained that the route from Banyuls—seven hours over the Pyrenees—circumvented Cerbère, the border station on the railroad and the coastal highway where German agents had been seen. It was being tested now by a young man who

would wire of his arrival in Lisbon before we set out. We
would get more specific directions in Banyuls, where a
French contact expected us at a certain bistro whose proprietor was reliable; we should identify ourselves by the torn
numbered card.

As far as our papers were concerned, I decided to hide my
American "affidavit in lieu of passport" and to show only the
Czech passport, on which I had the transit visas. Thus Carli
and I would carry similar papers, which seemed safer—especially for him.

Three days later Fry notified us that the wire from Lisbon
had come. It had taken the sender three days to travel
through Spain, with two overnight stops, in Barcelona and
Madrid. Each time we stopped, we knew, we would have to
leave our passports at the hotel desk. The only luggage Fry
would allow each of us to take was a beach bag; if we were
caught in France, we were to say that we were in Banyuls
to go swimming and had lost our way. And he cautioned us
to reach the border about noon, since the French patrols
were timed so as not to interfere with the sacred hour for
luncheon.

The beach bags reminded me: I really must have one more
swim at Pointe Rouge. It was a lovely day, and there might
never be another chance. Carli, in the meantime, could pick up
Hilde Walter in town, where she was staying—at a house
of ill repute, because the police at that time liked to take it
easy in such places and did not question the inmates.

My head was still wet from my swim when I came to the
Splendide to say goodbye to Mehring. "We'll never see each
other again," he muttered glumly.

And Varian Fry, dry-voiced and matter-of-fact as ever,
quickly slipped me my travel money and said, "See you in
New York," quite casually, to me too.

Then I met Carli and Hilde at the station, on the platform
for the Perpignan train. Traveling without safe conducts,
of course, we separated on the train to avoid attention;

safely in Perpignan, we joined up again. Hilde, it had been decided in the meantime, was to wait there for another group and take an easier route, if possible, because for her our new one seemed too strenuous.

Carli and I traveled on to Banyuls. We went to the bistro where we were to spend the night. The proprietor took our passports and said we would get them back the next day from the contact; we would find both him and our friends at the station, where he worked as a porter. "Number one hundred and seven," the innkeeper said. We invited him to have a bottle of wine with us, and the bottle turned into several; we spent half the night drinking together, and the man filled us with good advice.

In the morning I woke up with a terrible headache. I blamed the wine—until I started running a fever. I could hardly crawl, but at the innkeeper's suggestion Carli dragged me to a doctor, who diagnosed a bad cold and painted my tonsils with iodine, which seemed to make things worse. "That's what you get for swimming," Carli fumed. "Now you've got to wait here; as soon as I know the right way across the border, I'll come back for you, and tomorrow we go together."

When he came back, late at night, he found me unconscious on the floor, with no idea how I had fallen out of bed. He fed me aspirin and reported: Everything had gone perfectly. Porter No. 107 had been at the station with Muhlen, Natonek, the blonde, and our passports. He had explained the route; the only trick was to get to the right Spanish border post, where you had to present yourself and get an entry stamp in your passport. That made you *en règle* in Spain. Carli had watched the procedure from afar before turning back. He said Muhlen and Natonek seemed to have gone through all right, but the Czech girl had left under guard.

Later we heard that she had been concealing money on her person—in an unmentionable place—for which offense she

211

was promptly arrested. In the morning, however, the post commander himself let her out of her cell. *"Merci,"* she said.

He shook his head. *"C'est à moi de vous remercier, madame—I* have to thank *you,"* he said, in perfect French, and kept the money.

We were in no such danger, having little money left, but Carli said we couldn't stay any longer, since our passports had been returned. My legs rebelled at carrying me, but somehow we crept along behind the cemetery and up the dry riverbed to a spring where I could drink at last, on through vineyards, to the Norman tower. The noonday sun was blazing. I had to rest. Carli had brought food along, but I couldn't swallow a thing. Far beneath us lay the sea, as blue as the sky, and a town like a shadow on the rocky landscape: Cerbère, which we had to go around.

Carli grew impatient. "We've got to move on," he said. "We must be at the border before it gets dark, or I won't be able to find the place anymore."

I stumbled downhill, over rocks, and he had to support me. And then—I don't know how it happened—we ran too soon into the Spanish border patrol. It was the wrong one. They arrested us and took us to a post. They spoke no French; we could barely make ourselves understood. But on the floor of the guard room puppies were sprawling, three or four weeks old, and one of the Spaniards and I began to play with them. Suddenly I saw him laugh at me.

And Carli remembered the cigarettes Fry had given him in case of need, Gauloises Bleues and Gitanes Vertes. He started offering them to the Spaniards. Soon we were all smoking together, but it made me cough too much, and I fell asleep on the wooden bench.

In the morning we got our passports back, properly stamped, and were sent on our way. Carli could not turn back any more; he had to continue with me to Port-Bou, the rail station. Fry had warned me to travel first class because second and third were apt to be full of military personnel and dangerous; but the money I had, we discovered, would take two people to Lisbon in third class only. In a uniformed throng we pushed our way into a third-class car. The soldiers eyed us curiously, but when Carli started singing French student songs he knew, they quickly joined in even though they did not know the lyrics. As in the babel of the Sevareids' Parisian apartment, all nations seemed to understand each other, and in my feverish delirium I thought I could see the same writing on the wall. . . .

The boys in the Spanish uniforms waved to us when we got off in Barcelona. Perhaps they really were on our side. At the hotel where we registered, our Czech passports were taken away, and all through the night we feared being arrested; but in the morning we got the passports back and could go on. It was the same in Madrid.

On the fourth day rather than on the third, for the trains were slow, we finally came to the Portuguese frontier. As though by chance, the last required stamps were placed on our passports; an hour later the train pulled into Lisbon. There, looking out over the harbor, I suddenly felt it had all been a nightmare. Wasn't I still in Marseilles, with the fish-wives screeching at the Vieux Port? The fruits of the sea lay piled in towering baskets; the lobsters simmered in the pot. . . . Had I really escaped?

I felt sick during the hour-long search for a place to stay. Lisbon was overflowing with refugees; here, too, a garret was all that Carli could find, though it did not look quite as dilapidated as that of the late curé in Toulouse. My temperature rose to 104°, and I had to stay in bed. Carli went, first, to look up the young man whose telegram had been the signal for our departure. The young man was no longer registered at his hotel, and the concierge said his room was no longer available. We heard that he had killed himself in it shortly after his arrival—no one knew why.

Carli sent Fry a detailed report from Lisbon, explaining why he had been unable to turn back and enclosing correc-

tions for the map on thin paper. The letter arrived safely in
Marseilles, and thousands more managed to escape on Fry's
routes. Later, when the United States entered the war, the
same routes came to be used as entrances for agents of the
Office of Strategic Services.

I was still running a high fever when Carli found passage
for me on the *Nea Hellas*, a Greek ship on which the American committee had booked space for visa-holding refugees.
I did not want to take it; I begged Carli to let me recover
first, to let me rest awhile, but he insisted. No other ships
were sailing to America then, and Carli feared the Germans
might catch up with us even in Lisbon. I must cross the
Atlantic as I had crossed the Pyrenees, well or unwell.

Leaning half dazed on the ship's rail just before sailing, I
recognized Norbert Muhlen among my fellow passengers.
Carli was waving from the pier. He could not come along; he
had no visa. I was to try and get one for him in New York.

We sailed on the stroke of midnight, September 3–4, 1940
—one year after the declaration of war had been announced
over the loudspeaker in Clairac. Carli stood looking after us,
his figure shrinking as the *Nea Hellas* slowly turned down
the Tagus. The lights of the Lisbon World's Fair danced
astern; soon they were no more than a faint reddish glow.
Bloodred, Europe sank beneath the horizon.

CHAPTER 11

Out of Midnight

"Some may die on the way." Varian Fry used to quote what his faithful assistant Beamish had once said about their work: "Some will never get over it; some will be the better for the experience. But one must get them all out. At least one must try."

Two of Fry's aides lost their lives trying. Frederic Drach was found riddled with bullets; Charles Wolff disappeared. Later it was learned that he had died in a Gestapo torture chamber.

Fry himself saw some of his prize protégés across the border; with one party, made up of the Werfels, Heinrich Mann and his wife, and their nephew Golo, he went all the way to Lisbon. Miraculously—Mann was seventy, Werfel a cardiac case—these distinguished elderly writers managed the climb over the hills and dodged the French border patrols, only to be recognized at the Spanish police post. They thought they were lost, but fate had a quirk in store: "I am honored to make the acquaintance of the son of so great a man," a Franco border guard said to Thomas Mann's son Golo. What Heinrich Mann felt at the moment is not recorded.

Fry returned to Marseilles to continue his work. The trap kept tightening; he kept finding new ways out. Mary Jayne Gold, a young American beauty who in prewar days had flown her private plane all over Europe, proved invaluable for special jobs.

At the outbreak of the war she had presented her plane to the French government. When she came to volunteer for Fry, he found her "a made-to-order charmer." In fact, she once persuaded a concentration-camp chief to let four prisoners out to pick up their U.S. visas at Marseilles; once there, they were promptly spirited out of the country.

Fry himself helped the British to get out their soldiers interned near Marseilles; in exchange they enabled him to put his own charges on ships bound for Dakar or Casablanca. Most of the British soldiers swam ashore at Gibraltar.

Charles, a gangster confidant from the Dorade Bar, became an increasingly useful source of false papers and contacts at the border and in port. When Fry found a freighter due to sail directly overseas to Martinique or other French possessions, Fry decided to use this route for Breitscheid and Hilferding, the two men then in the greatest danger, who could not possibly go through Spain or Vichy-controlled North Africa.

Arrangements were made. Two bunks were waiting; but on the night before the sailing date Breitscheid and Hilferding vanished. Fry's French police contact shrugged and professed ignorance of their whereabouts. The U.S. consul personally called Vichy, but in vain. To the two top names on the "surrender" list, Paragraph 19 of the Armistice was applied verbatim.

Months later Fry learned that Hilferding, removed to the

Santé Prison in Paris, had been found hanged in his cell and pronounced a suicide. Word about Breitscheid came from German radio three years later: He was said to have died in an Allied bombing of Buchenwald. Fry was always convinced that both had been killed on Hitler's orders.

Some died on the way. . . .

America was not yet in the war when we landed at Hoboken, New Jersey, on September 12, 1940. At dawn, when the Statue of Liberty came into sight, we stood on deck, staring, and I wondered about the torch in the bronze woman's hand. I knew her only from literature and remembered that Franz Kafka had described her as bearing a sword.

Across the river the New York skyline loomed like a mountain chain, soaring from sea level into the clouds. Before we could approach it, we had to pass the immigration authorities. In my excitement I unfortunately forgot the magic formula we were supposed to recite: "I am a guest of the American Federation of Labor. . . ."

Unable to name anyone else who might promise to support me, I was about to be sent to Ellis Island, the place for arrivals whose papers were not in order—"*pas en règle,*" as this predicament had been known in France. I was informed that I would stay on the island until somebody came up with five hundred dollars bail for me. That would never happen, I knew, and burst into tears. I couldn't think of *anyone* in New York who had five hundred dollars.

A girl crying by the ship's rail, in plain view of everyone, seemed to disturb the orderly proceedings. Attempts were made to get me back below deck. At the last moment a man from the Rescue Committee spotted me from the pier. "What's the matter?" he called.

I shouted out my name. He was a former Austrian, Josef Buttinger, and he found my name on his list of scheduled arrivals. It took a while for him to straighten things out, but eventually I joined the others who had gone ashore.

217

They had a ring of reporters around them, but not for long. The press, it turned out, was not looking for writers. "Are there no aristocrats?" The question was flung at everybody who came down the gangplank, and soon we were left alone—which was better, for one thing that Fry had impressed on each of us above anything else was to say nothing about how we had escaped, for the sake of those left behind.

The next stop was customs. "Didn't you bring any luggage?" I was asked by an amazed inspector.

"Just my head," I answered, and he waved me through. "Thank you," I said.

His reply moved me deeply. It was "You're welcome," and I did not know as yet that in America you hear those words whenever you say "Thank you."

Behind the barrier we were greeted by Hermann Kesten. He no sooner saw me than he demanded, only half in jest, "How dare you come without Mehring?" It took a lot to convince him that Mehring had not wanted to go with us over the hills.

We drove through a long tunnel, and Kesten lodged us at his hotel in New York. It was fifteen stories high, across the street from the Museum of Natural History, with a friendly view of Central Park. To me it seemed a fairy castle. Theodore Dreiser had lived there, Kesten told us; now, besides himself and Toni, his wife, there were already a few more of us. Later there would also be Mehring and Leonhard Frank, on their way to Hollywood.

My ten dollars, all I had, sufficed for a week's rent, which came to nine. Then things got difficult. "You can't expect to be fed by people who have just pulled you out of the water," Kesten ventured and made me a loan of three dollars. In those days that was a lot. At the little Greek restaurant next to our hotel the daily menu hung in the window: Dinner—three whole courses—cost fifty cents; just as much as our cartoonist, Bill Freier, in Marseilles had received for false identity cards. I'll never forget it. For me in New York a fifty-cent dinner was a luxury I could not afford. I used to devour the three courses with my eyes, through the windowpane, before going to the bakery next door for two jelly doughnuts. They cost a nickel; it was the cheapest way to make yourself full.

The Rescue Committee gave us a welcome dinner at the Hotel Commodore, and in secondhand clothes—they were almost new—that we got from another committee I was able to attend. There was more food than I had seen in a week. Eleanor Roosevelt spoke; she was our hostess.

She had spoken to the President in our behalf, and therefore we had been permitted to enter the United States. Now she was speaking to us. Her words have been guiding me ever since. "I never look back," the First Lady explained. She always looked only forward so that she could find out what *ought* to be done—that's why she was able to achieve so many things.

Then each of us was supposed to say a few words in reply. I stammered that to express my gratitude was . . . I stopped, searched for the word I wanted, could not find it in English, and finally said it in French: "*impossible.*" Laughter, applause—I was stunned. I had no idea that the word was the same in both languages and that I had simply been saying it with a French accent.

I understood something Dorothy Thompson told us that evening, though. "We can use even your nervous breakdown," the famed journalist said, and this line too is still etched in my mind.

Nervous breakdown? I wondered. At the time we were so happy to be saved that nothing else seemed to bother us. Only when the fire sirens screeched at night, as happened often, would I wake up in panic, looking wildly for cover from Nazi planes. And every day, for only a nickel, we rode across town to the Rescue Committee's East Side office to find out what could be done for the ones still trapped abroad.

We noticed that little about them appeared in the papers, and I started writing down what was so fresh in my memory —the details of my flight from Paris to Marseilles—up to the unprintable part involving Fry and his work. This was still about a year before Pearl Harbor. Muhlen found me a little old typewriter that was cheap because some keys were missing and certain letters had to be inserted by hand. When the article was done, I took it to an agent who knew German. He said he would have it translated and gave me ten dollars, emphasizing that this was not an advance but a small "contribution." The translation never materialized, so I sold the piece to a new German-language weekly whose top fee for articles was five dollars. Mine was run in three installments, so I got fifteen dollars.

This could not go on, I heard from the relief committee that provided small sums for our support. I had to get a job, and one was actually found for me, as a maid in New Jersey. Having been rescued because I was a writer evidently was no reason to remain one.

It was then that I made my mistake, being woefully backward in American ways. I knew even then that I was very bad at housework, but instead of letting the lady in New Jersey discover that for herself and throw me out, I tried to explain it to the committee. As a result, the committee threw me out instead. Today I would know better.

Utterly lost, I stood there, near the committee offices, between the skyscrapers. My only way out seemed to be to jump off the top of Rockefeller Center, but I had not even the money to get up to the Observation Roof. Besides, I could not find the place in my confusion. I walked round and round for I don't know how long, thinking over how bad it might be to end that way after having been rescued and brought to this country so miraculously.

Finally I saw a familiar house in front of me. It was the address of a couple who had written to me after my article appeared, and I suddenly remembered that I had been invited there for that evening. I knew I looked a fright, but I went up anyway. My hosts were wonderful. They fed me and calmed me down, and when I was leaving, another guest whom I had hardly noticed said he would like to talk to me. We went on to a café, and he offered me a job.

His name was Willy Ley. Later he became one of America's leading experts on space flight; the subject had fasci nated him from boyhood on, and as a student in Germany ne had worked on a prophetic "moon shot" motion picture. In 1940 he was making twenty-seven dollars a week as science editor of a New York daily. The paper threatened to fold any day, so Willy laid the ground for a new career by writing science fiction. My job was to type his manuscripts for nine dollars a week.

It covered my rent exactly, and I felt in the clouds. The only trouble was that half of what I typed was Greek to me, or worse. I had to type some pages twenty times before they made any sense at all, quite apart from misspellings. Willy would return them with mistakes marked in red, as in elementary school. Only an angel's patience could have made him keep me on the job at all, and the worst thing he would say to me in moments of despair was: "Hertha, you are going to end on the junk pile."

I did begin to learn English, however. Progress was slow, but the red marks diminished. Above all, Willy took me to the movies—way downtown near Times Square, where admission was a quarter, performances were continuous, and you could stay as long as you pleased. I remember sitting through two successive showings of *Gone with the Wind*, and I still think that besides my typing that was the best way for me to learn English at the moment.

By Christmastime, 1940—my first in America—I no longer thought about jumping off the top of Rockefeller Center. I walked past it, listening happily to the tune that loudspeakers sent down from the tall building as though straight from heaven: "Silent night, holy night. . . ." It felt like a greeting from home.

Walking by my side, in uniform, was an old acquaintance. America was still at peace, but American volunteers were flying with the British Royal Air Force, and many more were enlisting back home. The letter I had written to Minnesota after my arrival had reached Lieutenant Ted Meltzer in an army camp on the East Coast, and on his next New York furlough he had looked me up.

"Silent Night" faded away. "That song comes from Austria, like me," I said to Ted, although I thought he knew it.

He did not. " 'Silent Night'? That's an old American folk song." And when I gasped, he chuckled. "Not all good music has to come from Austria."

"This does." I told him the story of the carol: how it was born near Salzburg and went all over the world, and how in Europe too it was considered a folk song until chance—or a miracle—brought the composer to light, a humble, far-from-famous Alpine choirmaster who marveled more than anyone at the great strides his little song had taken.

"You must write that story," said Ted Meltzer.

I wrote it as an article, got Willy Ley to check it for English mistakes, and started sending it to magazines. American magazines were plentiful in those days, and the piece came back from everywhere. After some twenty rejections I gave up. There were more important things to be done.

The Rescue Committee had exciting news one day: through Josef Buttinger, my "rescue angel" from the pier, I got confirmation that Carli was on the emergency visa list. Eric Sevareid had signed the necessary affidavit, and now Carli's visa had arrived. The remaining difficulties—passage money, a ship, a berth—were ironed out in a matter of weeks, and Carli sailed from Lisbon to Norfolk, Virginia.

In Norfolk he was stopped by the Immigration Service, which had no experience with any refugees. Everyone else disembarked; Carli had to stay on the freighter. In a few days the ship would return to Europe, with him aboard.

On the last day a telegram reached Eric Sevareid, who ran all the way from his office to Western Union to send money and the further endorsement required by the authorities. Later, Sevareid described the reunion that followed. At one of their rushed encounters in France he had given Carli an old sleeping bag; he had forgotten all about it until Carli stood in the door, smiling and holding out a dirty roll of khaki cloth. "You see, I have brought back your sleeping bag. I think in America there'll be no need. . . ."

In New York Carli and I had only a short time together. It was the policy of the committees to "resettle" refugees away from the metropolis where so many had gathered already, and Carli was sent to work on a Quaker farm in Indiana. Soon after his departure I got a call: The Rescue Committee had a message for me. I found a bulky envelope, addressed in Walter Mehring's handwriting and postmarked Martinique. I tore it open, looked for a letter, found none— the envelope contained nothing but a sheaf of manuscripts.

"*Letters out of Midnight*," said the title page, "by Walter Mehring." They were twelve poems, begun in Vienna, continued in French internment camps and on the flight that we had made together, completed in Marseilles. It was our story from 1937 to 1941, the one long night in which time broke asunder—and here I had it in my hands, addressed to me, held fast in a thousand and one lines.

Without comment.

"Come soon," I wrote back. And he came, having flown from the French Antilles to Miami and continued by train. Fry had sent him to Martinique on the freighter *Wyoming*, with war cargo and colonial troops, in the berth that had been meant for Rudolf Hilferding.

"What do we do now?" Walter asked when I met him at Pennsylvania Station.

I took him straight from the underground train tracks into the subway; he did not see daylight until we came up the stairs by the edge of Central Park. "Take a look first," I

223

said. And for a while we just stood there, gazing at the sky-scrapers above the trees.

Walter had been right. The mirage, the miracle he had pre-dicted, promised, sworn to me, in the roadside ditches of France when I thought I could not walk another step—it had come true. We were in America, both of us. "The one good thing Hitler did," we used to say, "was to bring us to this country." It was not Hitler who really did it, though: It was Varian Fry.

At a party in 1942 we saw him again. Except for the gray-flannel suit he wore instead of slacks and shirt sleeves, he looked the same as at our first encounter; but here he was one among many. Nothing in the Buster Keaton face indicated that he was the guest of honor. His reserve seemed mere shyness, lacking the old mystery. When we drank to him, silently because we found no words, it was as if he were not really with us, not part of the crowd, but somehow still far away. Of him, as of us, a part had remained in Marseilles. And just as we never got over that time when he had snatched us from the grip of death, he seemed not to have found his way back to everyday life from his great adventure.

Casually he asked what we were doing now. We were writ-ing—and so, it turned out, was he, and about us. He had be-gun a book on his work in Marseilles, titled *Surrender on Demand.*

I told him of the poems Mehring had written there, and Mehring added that his latest, written in New York, was called "Rescue Visa." It would probably never be printed, Mehring said, and this led to my telling the troubles of my "Silent Night" piece. A woman was passing by, and Fry stopped her: "Listen to this, Lillian."

When I had finished, she smiled and said, "That is a chil-dren's book." She was Lillian Bragdon, juvenile editor of Knopf, and she taught me all I know about writing for children. My little book was lovingly published by her, and the story that had been turned down by every magazine ran

in the *Reader's Digest* at Christmastime, 1943, like a faint
note of peace amid the din of war.

Fry's manuscript lay hidden in a drawer. "To have written
about my work while the Gestapo was still in France," he
later explained, "would have been to betray friends to im-
prisonment and possibly to death." When he finally published
the book after the war's end, interest was drawn away from it
by the new tide of refugees whom the Rescue Committee was
helping across the Atlantic.

Fry moved restlessly from job to job, from the League for
the Rights of Man to the Foreign Policy Association, to the
Labor Conference on International Affairs, to the editorial
chairs of various journals. It did not satisfy him to switch
from action to words, however. Later he sought distraction
in Latin crossword puzzles, and to ease the strain of settling
down he studied the ways of migratory birds.

When, over twenty years later, he was belatedly awarded
the French Legion of Honor, I sent him a letter of congratu-
lations, wondering whether he still remembered me. He replied at once.

```
      Of course I remember you--well. And I still
have the copy of Silent Night you gave me,
with a very flattering inscription: "To Varian
Fry, our 'Saviour'--Thankfully, H.P."
      Yes, it has been a long time, hasn't it?
Sometimes I wonder where my life has gone. . . .
      You have done much better than I in those
twenty-two years: You have published about
twenty books, while I have published none. I
have been writing--but mostly for business,
and so almost always anonymously. . . .
      By all means try to telephone me. . . .
      And thank you for writing.
                          Sincerely,
                          Varian Fry
                          19 April 1967
```

Soon after, we met at the Harvard Club in New York. His face looked older but as inscrutable as ever. He talked of the need to communicate with young people. He wanted to rewrite *Surrender on Demand* as a juvenile and to move to Connecticut and become a Latin teacher. His wife and children would remain in New York.

The absentminded eyes went past me. "What are a thousand rescued people?" And then, matter-of-factly: "One should save millions from death by terror."

On September 14, 1967, Norbert Muhlen called me: Varian, he said, had been found dead in the new home he had recently moved to in Easton, Connecticut. He had died of a heart attack, apparently, though no one was quite sure. The man who had saved two thousand lives had died alone, at fifty-nine years of age.

"An unsung hero died," said the obituaries that brought him back from oblivion. They recalled his rescue of "such notables as Heinrich Mann, novelist and brother of Thomas Mann; Marc Chagall, artist; Jacques Lipchitz, sculptor; Franz Werfel, poet and dramatist; Wanda Landowska, musician; Dr. Otto Meyerhof, Nobel Prize–winning scientist. . . ." The list filled half a column. "An entire culture in exile owes Varian Fry its survival."

At a memorial in New York Jacques Lipchitz spoke *to* Fry, not about him. "Varian," he said, "we won't forget you as long as we live; but even long after we are gone, you'll be remembered."

We remember you, Varian Fry. You and all those you helped are inseparable, for you unlocked our door to a new life. . . .

Our house stands behind a twenty-five-foot privet hedge. It faces a lawn with fruit trees and an old barn and woods in back forming an undulating horizon. The view from my window often used to make me think of the Vienna Woods.

I used to go visiting across the road, on what was once an estate on a hilltop. The former main house is now a nursing home, and for a time I was privileged to go there to read the newspapers to a great, virtually blind old man—Norman Thomas. He had spent a lifetime fighting for change in America, and yet to me he seemed continuity personified, a tall, gaunt embodiment of the American Image we cherished, of the old American dream: liberty and justice for all and the pursuit of happiness in peace. . . .

In the fifties, before there was a nursing home, I used to visit at the former carriage house across the road, an immense place that had been converted into an artist's studio. The artist was George Grosz. His had been a name to conjure with in the Berlin of my early acting days, but I had met him only here, after the war, through Walter Mehring. They were old friends from the German Dada movement, and Mehring came often from New York to visit him.

Grosz had left Germany in 1932, before Hitler came to power, to teach at the Art Students League in New York. America was his childhood dream; he knew all the old books about cowboys and Indians. Over here the acid pen and brush that had seared the rot of Germany became bucolic, returning only now and then to the impending Apocalypse, to Nazi boots and blood and war. When television came in, George would spend hours before the set each day, watching Westerns.

We always sat in the vine-covered pergola behind Grosz's house, he and Mehring and I. American critics had raved over Mehring's book *The Lost Library: Autobiography of a Culture*, in which, framed into a narrative, the author rebuilt his father's library. I had published a score of books too, most of them dealing with people, things, and ideas that are at home in America but came from abroad, as I did. In between, though, I had turned to American history, as in *Lincoln's Little Correspondent* or the biography of the famous freed slave of Lincoln's time, Sojourner Truth, the woman whose way of life marked the fight for the equality of men and women of today.

As we sat in George Grosz's vine-covered pergola, we

often talked of our friends, both the ones who had made it and the ones who had not, and sometimes Walter and I spoke of the years in France, of which Grosz knew only what he had heard others tell. He would put his feet on the table and growl at Walter and me, pointing at the soles of his shoes. "See the rootlets down there? I have grown roots in America. You? You've never arrived here. You are all still in Marseilles."

There was some truth in it. We got out of the trap like foxes who nevertheless leave a piece of leg behind. At the end of the fifties, however, Grosz tore up his rootlets, sold his beloved carriage house on the hilltop, and returned to Berlin, only to die there shortly after, falling down his stairway at night.

My new life here is now over thirty years old. The cherries are in bloom again before my window; there is a breeze from the Sound, and the wooded horizon no longer looks like the Vienna Woods, which I usually visit every year. George Grosz was not altogether wrong: A part of me— as of Varian Fry, of those who helped him, and of those he rescued—is still European. Time broke in two in those frightful, wonderful days. . . .

As one of the few survivors I have now tried to hold fast what happened thirty years ago, to span the break that then occurred in our time—the heartbreak of our world.

Appendix

Biographical Data

Chagall, Marc, painter; b. Vitebsk, Russia, 1887. Avant-garde movements Paris (1910), Berlin, Moscow; 1922 to France to stay; French citizen; to United States 1941–1947, again in 1960's (Lincoln Center murals, New York City). Lives in France and Israel.

Csokor, Franz Theodor, dramatist; b. Vienna, Austria, 1885. Early Expressionist poet, later foremost Austrian classicist. Exile 1938, in protest against Anschluss; World War II flight through Poland, Roumania, Yugoslavia, Italy; 1945, back to Vienna; president Austrian PEN. Published in English: *A Civilian in the Polish War* (1940). Died Vienna, 1969.

Feuchtwanger, Lion, novelist; b. Munich, Germany, 1884. One of most popular German authors in 1920's; exile 1933, when Hitler came to power; since 1940 in United States. Published in English: *Power* (1929) and many other novels. Died Pacific Palisades, California, 1951.

Grosz, George, painter; b. Stolp, Germany (now Poland), 1893. In Dada movement after World War I; in 1920's foremost political and social satirist in European art, he was tried for blasphemy after drawing Christ with gas mask; 1932, guest teacher at New York Art Students League, stayed in United States after Nazi takeover in Germany; member American Institute of Arts and Letters. Back to Berlin June, 1959; died there three weeks later.

Gumbel, Emil J., mathematical statistician; b. Munich, Germany, 1891. Active pacifist; 1924, as assistant professor in Heidelberg, center of a storm about "insulting German war dead"; exile 1933; professor at University of Lyons, France; after 1940

229

taught in United States (Columbia University and New School for Social Research, New York City). Died New York City, 1966.

Hasenclever, Walter, playwright; b. Aachen, Germany, 1890. Early Expressionist poet; later successful chiefly with Noel Coward–type comedies; active pacifist. Exile 1933. Suicide, Camp Les Milles, France, 1940.

Heiden, Konrad, contemporary historian; b. Munich, Germany, 1901. Correspondent and editorial writer for leading German newspapers; exile 1933; since 1940 in United States, where his Hitler biography *Der Fuehrer* (1944) was number-one nonfiction best-seller. Died New York City, 1967.

Hirschmann, Albert O. ("Beamish"), economist; b. Berlin, Germany, 1915. In 1930's student (Paris, London) and Spanish Civil War volunteer; since 1940 in United States (Rockefeller Fellow, Berkeley; G.I.; Federal Reserve Board aide; professor at Yale, Columbia, since 1964 Harvard, universities). Lives in Cambridge, Massachusetts.

Horvath, Odon von, playwright and novelist; b. Fiume, Austria-Hungary (now Yugoslavia), 1901. Raised Budapest and Munich; early 1930's in Berlin, won top German drama award, work attacked by Nazis; now revived throughout German-language area as precursor of today's avant-garde. Published in English: *The Age of the Fish* and *A Child of Our Time* (novels, 1939). Died Paris, 1938.

Kesten, Hermann, novelist; b. Nuremberg, Germany, 1900. Exile 1933; May, 1940 (just before German invasion of France), to New York City. Devoted years to full-time refugee rescue effort; recent work mainly to save memory and spirit of the literature Nazis sought to kill. Published in English: *I, the King* (1939) and many other novels, biographies, anthologies. Lives alternately in New York City and Rome.

Lipchitz, Jacques, sculptor; b. Druskieniki, Russia (now Soviet Lithuania), 1891. Parisian avant-garde 1909; 1941 to United States; now modeling monumental sculptures for Columbia University. Lives in Hastings-on-Hudson, New York, and Italy.

Mann, Heinrich, novelist; b. Lubeck, Germany, 1871. As widely read as his brother Thomas in pre-Nazi Germany (especially

230

after a story of his was filmed as *The Blue Angel*); president Prussian Academy of Letters; lifelong antimilitarist, active anti-Nazi. Exile 1933; since 1940 in United States. Published in English: *Henry of Navarre* (1938 best-seller) and many others. Died Santa Monica, California, 1950.

Mann, Thomas, novelist; b. Lubeck, Germany, 1875. Since 1929, when he received Nobel Prize, considered foremost living representative of German literature. A self-styled nonpolitical man, he opposed the Nazis as a humanist and exiled himself, 1933 to Switzerland, 1938 to United States, 1948 back to Switzerland. Published in English: virtually all of his works. Died Zurich, 1955.

Mehring, Walter, poet; b. Berlin, Germany, 1896. Original Dadaist, political satirist, a twentieth-century François Villon. In 1920's alternately in Berlin and Paris; 1941 to United States; 1953 back to Germany, later Switzerland. Published in English: *No Road Back* (poems, 1944), *The Lost Library: Autobiography of a Culture* (1951). Lives in Zurich.

Morgenstern, Soma, novelist and journalist; b. Volhynia, Austria-Hungary (now Soviet Ukraine), 1896. Viennese literary correspondent; exile 1938; since 1941 in United States. Published in English: *The Son of the Lost Son* (1946). Lives in New York City.

Muhlen, Norbert, journalist; b. Fuerth, Germany, 1909. Active in anti-Nazi German student organization until 1933; in exile after 1935 Saar resistance to Nazis; since 1940 in United States. Regular contributor to many United States and German newspapers and magazines. Published in English: *The Incredible Krupps* (1959) and others. Lives in New York City.

Natonek, Hans, novelist and journalist; b. Prague, Austria-Hungary (now Czechoslovakia), 1892. With German newspapers until 1933; home to Prague; exile 1938; since 1940 in United States. Published in English: *In Search of Myself* (autobiography, 1944). Died Tucson, Arizona, 1963.

Roth, Joseph, novelist; b. Schwabendorf, Austria-Hungary (now Soviet Ukraine), 1894. World War I Austrian officer; later contributor to leading Viennese and German papers; novels (since 1924) today rediscovered as classics of German prose and Austrian tradition. Published in English: *Job* (1931, translated by Dorothy Thompson) and many other novels. Died Paris, 1939.

Sahl, Hans, poet and translator; b. Dresden, Germany, 1902. In 1920's Berlin's youngest drama and film critic; exile 1933; since 1941 in U.S.; now foremost German translator of American plays (Thornton Wilder, Arthur Miller, Tennessee Williams) and correspondent for leading German and Swiss papers. Published in English: *The Few and the Many* (novel, 1962). Lives in New York City.

Toller, Ernst, poet and playwright; b. Samotchin, Germany (now Poland), 1893. Expressionist and revolutionary; influence on German stage anticipating Brecht's; abroad 1933, kept barnstorming Europe and United States against fascism. Published in English: *The Swallow Book* (poems written in prison after abortive 1919 Munich coup, 1924), *Seven Plays* (1934), and others. Suicide, New York City, 1939.

Torberg, Friedrich, novelist and journalist; b. Prague, Austria-Hungary (now Czechoslovakia), 1908. In 1930's in Vienna, striking success with first novel, friendship with Franz Werfel; exile 1938; Czech Army in France; 1941–1950 in United States (Los Angeles, New York City); 1954–1965 founder-editor *Forum* magazine, Vienna; collected works now appearing. Lives in Breitenfurth, near Vienna.

Walter, Hilde, journalist; b. Berlin, Germany, 1895. Associate editor of Karl von Ossietzky's liberal magazine *Weltbühne* until 1933; in exile compaigned to win 1935 Nobel Peace Prize for Ossietzky (then in Nazi concentration camp); 1940 to United States. Published in English: *Conscience in Revolt* (contributor, 1957); since 1952 contributing to United States and German newspapers. Lives alternately in New York City and Berlin.

Weiss, Ernst, novelist; b. Brünn, Austria-Hungary (now Brno, Czechoslovakia), 1884. M.D. in Prague, friend of Franz Kafka and Franz Werfel; after World War I in Berlin until 1933; home to Prague; exile 1938; called "one of the outstanding European novelists of our time" (Hermann Kesten). Published in English: "Cardiac Suture" (short story) in *Heart of Europe* (anthology, 1943). Suicide, Paris, 1940.

Werfel, Alma Mahler; b. Vienna, Austria, 1879. Daughter of

painter Emil Schindler; widow of composer Gustav Mahler; divorced from architect Walter Gropius; married Franz Werfel in 1929 and accompanied him into exile (1938 France, 1940 United States). Published in English: *And the Bridge Is Love* (autobiography, 1959). Died New York City, 1964.

Werfel, Franz, novelist and playwright; b. Prague, Austria-Hungary (now Czechoslovakia), 1890. A leading Expressionist after World War I; later perhaps the German-language writer most successful in uniting literary quality with popular appeal. Published in English: *The Song of Bernadette* (1942 number-one best-seller) and almost all his other novels and plays. Died Santa Barbara, California, 1945.

Wittlin, Joseph, novelist and poet; b. Dmytrov, Austria-Hungary (now Poland), 1896. Fellow student of Joseph Roth; after World War I professor of Polish literature, Lvov; later headed state theater, Lodz; 1927 to Warsaw; exile 1939; since 1941 in United States. Published in English: *Salt of the Earth* (1941) and other novels. Lives in New York City.

Zernatto, Guido, poet and politician; b. in Carinthia, Austria, 1903. In 1930's secretary general of Austrian Fatherland Front, cabinet member, author of several books of poetry; 1938 adventurous flight to France; 1940 to United States; professor of Fordham University, published books on Austrian politics. Died in New York City, 1943.

Index

Index

237

Index

239